Svetlana Silova

Way of the Cross

Svetlana Silova

Way of the Cross

Patriotic activity of the Orthodox clergy in Belarus during the Great Patriotic War (1941-1945).

ScienciaScripts

Imprint

Any brand names and product names mentioned in this book are subject to trademark, brand or patent protection and are trademarks or registered trademarks of their respective holders. The use of brand names, product names, common names, trade names, product descriptions etc. even without a particular marking in this work is in no way to be construed to mean that such names may be regarded as unrestricted in respect of trademark and brand protection legislation and could thus be used by anyone.

Cover image: www.ingimage.com

This book is a translation from the original published under ISBN 978-3-659-81198-2.

Publisher:
Sciencia Scripts
is a trademark of
Dodo Books Indian Ocean Ltd. and OmniScriptum S.R.L publishing group

120 High Road, East Finchley, London, N2 9ED, United Kingdom
Str. Armeneasca 28/1, office 1, Chisinau MD-2012, Republic of Moldova, Europe
Printed at: see last page
ISBN: 978-620-8-14696-2

With the blessing of His Eminence PHILARETA

Metropolitan of Minsk and Slutsk, Patriarchal Exarch of All Belarus

Silova S.V. CREST PATH: THE BELORUSIAN ORTHODOX CHURCH IN THE PERIOD OF THE GERMAN OCCUPATION 1941-1944 G.G.

The book contains information about some aspects of church life in occupied Belarus, characterizes and gives numerous examples of patriotic activities of the Belarusian Orthodox clergy during the Great Patriotic War.

In preparing the text for publication, the author undertook a labor to eliminate many errors that, unfortunately, took place in the book: *S.V. Silova. The Way of the Cross. Orthodox Clergy in Belarus during the Great Patriotic War 1941-1945. Mn. 2004.*, as well as supplemented it with unique information of factual nature.

Designed for those interested in the history of our Fatherland.

Silova S.V.

Scientific Editor Sheikin G.N.

TABLE OF CONTENTS

FROM THE AUTHOR

The further away from us the events of the past are, the more objectively we can analyze them. The Second World War claimed the lives of every third inhabitant of Belarus. Our republic experienced the horror of Nazi occupation. Now we are thinking more and more about the source of moral and mental strength of the people who remained in the occupation and who strived not only to survive, but also to fight. There is no doubt that an important place in the moral support of the population was occupied by the Orthodox Church, the temple during the years of occupation was one of the few places where a person could turn to the Lord with a prayer for those who fought at the fronts, for those who were in the partisans, for those whose fate was unknown. The scanty reports of the Sovinformburo hid the horror, pain and hope that the population of Belarus lived with from June 1941 to July 1944.

To this day, assessments of the role of the Orthodox Church in various historical periods are not unambiguous. This fully applies to the period 1941-1945 . Representatives of the Soviet

In the history school, those who studied various aspects and aspects of the Great Patriotic War did not consider church problems, knowingly defining the role of the Orthodox Church as reactionary and the policy pursued by representatives of the Orthodox clergy as aiding and abetting the Nazi regime. But it was with the outbreak of the Great Patriotic War that the patriotic orientation of the Orthodox Church's activities became evident, which had also never before been the subject of serious research. Orthodox clergymen fought on the fronts of the Great Patriotic War, participated in the partisan and underground movement in Belarus, gave their lives for the victory over Nazism. We should also remember the pastoral and humanitarian activities of the clergy who remained with their parishioners in the occupation. It is necessary to remember all this and to know that the Orthodox clergy fully shared the bitter fate of all those who survived the war.

The history of our state is complex, interesting and contradictory. For many centuries, the territory of the present state - the Republic of Belarus - was part of various state formations and was called by different names. The author reserves the right to use the term "Belarus" as part of the name "Belarusian USSR", a part of the USSR, a state formation that existed at the time of the events described.

For the convenience of the reader, the author uses the modern territorial-administrative division of the Republic of Belarus.

The author will be grateful to everyone who has and is ready to share materials about the help provided by Orthodox priests to partisans and underground fighters in occupied Belarus. Please send your feedback to Svetlana Vladimirovna Silova at the address: 9 Brikel St., Brickel St., Grodno, 230005, apartment 42.

Chapter 1

The Situation of the Orthodox Church in Belorussia in 1941-1944.

The events of the Great Patriotic War are getting farther and farther away from us. Several generations have already been born who do not know the howling of air raid sirens, the whistling of bullets and shells. We take the peaceful sky above our heads for granted, and the golden poppies of Orthodox churches as something permanent and immutable. But the Soviet period of the existence of our republic was one of the most tragic in the history of the Orthodox Church. The Bolshevik Party, which came to power in October 1917, chose militant atheism as its official policy. In the eastern part of Belarus, which had been part of the Soviet Union since 1922, church and parish life was completely destroyed in the course of the monstrous persecution by the Soviet authorities. By 1939 all churches and monasteries were closed, since 1936 there was no archpastoral care, and practically all clergy were subjected to repressions. Many of the clergy were martyred. In Western Belorussia, which was part of the Polish state until September 1939, despite the persecution there, many churches continued to hold services. According to statistics, by June 1941, 542 Orthodox churches were functioning within the then BSSR. All of them were located in Western Belarus.

In May-June 1945 there were more than a thousand churches in Belorussia, 625 of them were registered. So what happened from June 1941 to June 1945 in Belarus? What led to the revival of the Orthodox Church? Why do some historians call this period "the second baptism of Russia"?

It is quite clear that Hitler did not seek the church's good, on the contrary, he emphasized: "... our policy in the broad Russian expanse must be to encourage any and every form of disunion and schism" [23, p. 92] [23, c. 92]. However, in the initial period of the war (June-August 1941), the Nazis paid little attention to church issues. Obviously, they were not prepared for the mass and spontaneous opening of churches by the people of God. The commanders of the advanced units of the Wehrmacht allowed the opening of churches without paying attention to the pro-patriarchal (meaning the Mother Church - the Moscow Patriarchate headed by Metropolitan Sergius (Stragorodsky), the Patriarchal Locum Tenens) orientation of the clergy and parishioners. But already in the fall of 1941 began a period of strict control and regulation of the activities of the Orthodox Church in occupied Belarus. In the General Commissariat of Belarus in Minsk, which was headed by Wilhelm Kube, a policy department was created. The official Leopold Jurda, who headed it, carried out the Nazi policies towards the Church. Already in October 1941, the General Commissariat of Belorussia declared that the Orthodox Church in Belorussia could exist only as an autocephalous church. On October 3, 1941 a message was sent to Metropolitan Panteleimon (Roznhevsky), which indicated not only the need to create an autocephalous church in Belarus, but also stipulated its name - "Belarusian Autocephalous Orthodox National Church" [75, f.15]. [75, л.15].

Photo. Metropolitan Panteleimon (Roznhevsky). Photo from the author's personal archive.

All priests, rectors of church parishes were ordered, as it had been practiced before, to compile clergy lists, i.e. to provide data on the state of the church, clergy and parish, to fill out personal questionnaires of priests and psalmists. All priests and clergy had to register with the occupation authorities. The Orthodox clergy had no right of free movement on the territory of Belarus. All these facts testify to the strict control of the occupation authorities over the activities of the Orthodox Church in the occupied territory.

Some Belarusian national figures who actively cooperated with the occupation regime also tried to control the church life. In an incomprehensible way they supposed to use the brute force of this regime for the establishment of Belarusian national principles! They tried to urgently involve also the Orthodox Church in their dreamed cause of the Belarusian national revival. They cared little for the observance of the internal canonical order of the Church. There was a constant conflict between them and the Orthodox episcopate, one of the main tasks of which is the strict observance of the Church canons, concerning their influence on the adoption by the episcopate of decisions of purely ecclesiastical-canonical importance. Thus, for example, they insisted on the accelerated Belarusization of the Orthodox Church, advocated the immediate declaration of autocephaly; through the drafting of numerous memoranda of ultimatum character and attempts to create a certain supra-church body, they sought to direct and control the inner church life.

Vladyka Panteleimon (Rozhnovsky), who was at the head of the Church, was able to convene a council of bishops on March 3, 1942, at which it was decided to divide Belarus into six dioceses: 1). Vitebsk, headed by Bishop Athanasius (Martos) of Vitebsk-Polotsk; 2). Grodno, headed by Bishop Venedikt (Bobkovsky) of Grodno-Belostok; 3). Minsk, headed by Metropolitan Panteleimon (Rozhnovsky) of Minsk and All Belarus; 4). Mogilev, headed by Bishop Philotheus (Narko) of Mogilev and Mstislavl; 5). Novogrudsk, headed by Bishop Veniamin (Novitsky) of Novogrudsk; 6). Smolensk, headed by Bishop Simeon (Sevbo) of Smolensk [80, l. 67].

Photo. Bishop Athanasius Martos, Archbishop Venedikt Bobkovsky, Bishop Gregory Borishkevich (from left to right)

Photo. Bishop Athanasius (Martos), Archbishop Venedikt (Bobkovsky), Bishop Gregory (Borishkevich) (left to right). Photo from the author's personal archive.

The occupation authorities, knowing about the pro-patriarchal orientation of Metropolitan Panteleimon, went to a clear violation of the canons of the Orthodox Church, which prohibit secular authorities from interfering in the decision of purely ecclesiastical issues. The occupation authorities simply physically removed him from the leadership of the metropolis. At the end of May 1942 the Metropolitan was summoned to the General Commissariat of Belarus, where Leopold Jurda officially announced the removal of Metropolitan Panteleimon (Roznowski) and the necessity of transferring the management of church affairs to Archbishop Philotheus (Narko). Metropolitan Panteleimon filed a protest, but it was rejected. He was ordered to prepare for departure to Lyady [63, p. 276], where he stayed until the fall of 1942, and for the winter period the German authorities moved him to the city of Vileika under the supervision of the German military police.

Photo. Archbishop Philotheus (Narco). Photo from the funds of the Belarusian State Archive of Film and Photo Documents (BGAKFD).

Church building in the territory of the Grodno and Bialystok dioceses was somewhat different. After these territories were annexed to East Prussia, they came under the jurisdiction of Metropolitan Seraphim (Lyada) of Berlin. On January 5, 1942 Archbishop Venedikt (Bobkowski) and Eugene Kotovich arrived from Zhirovitsky Monastery to the city of Hrodna to organize church life.

Initially the creation of the Gomel diocese was not planned. But on May 28, 1943, a congress of clergy was held in the city of Gomel, at which it was decided to ask Metropolitan Panteleimon (Rozhnovsky) to approve an independent diocese in the Gomel region. The petition was granted. In April, 1944 the Brest-Polessky diocese was attached to the Belarusian

8

Metropolitanate. Thus, the Belarusian Orthodox Church had eight dioceses.

An important and in its own way instructive page of church building on the territory of occupied Belarus was the attempt to declare autocephaly and to create a self-proclaimed "Belarusian Autocephalous Orthodox National Church". The realization of this idea pursued, first of all, the purpose of detachment of the Belarusian flock from the Mother Church - the Moscow Patriarchate, which fully corresponded to the instructions of A. Hitler. The work in this direction in many respects determined the church policy of the occupation authorities and their henchmen. Under direct German pressure the question of autocephaly was put to the All-Belarusian Council of the Orthodox Church, which was solemnly opened on August 30, 1942 in Minsk Spaso-Preobrazhensky Monastery. "All-Belarusian" this council can be called only conditionally, for the entire Belarusian Orthodox Church was not represented at it. Its convocation was inspired by the occupation authorities with full organizational support for this event. The absence among the delegates of the legitimate Primate of the Church Metropolitan Panteleimon (Rozhnevsky), who was actually under arrest by the Germans, drew attention. The occupation authorities did not allow him to return to Minsk. Under their pressure, the Metropolitan transferred in writing all the powers to conduct the Council to Archbishop Philotheus (Narko). The Council proclaimed the establishment of the autocephaly of the Belarusian Orthodox Church and adopted its Statute. In paragraph 113 of this document it was stated that the canonical declaration of autocephaly would follow after its recognition by all Local Orthodox Churches [107]. This suggests that autocephaly was proclaimed formally, quite possibly even to reduce the degree of pressure on the episcopate by the occupation administration. Subsequently, the documents of the Council never received canonical approval and recognition by the entire Church Fullness. Nor could they receive it, for they were adopted under pressure from the secular, and even foreign, occupation authorities. In 1941-1944 one of the most difficult problems to solve was the question of personnel. While in the western regions of Belarus there was no special need for priests, in the central and eastern regions there was a great shortage of them. It was necessary to create educational institutions to train clergymen in a short time. Courses were opened to train candidates for priestly and clergy positions in the cities of Minsk, Grodno, Novogrudok, Gomel, Vitebsk (in 1942 up to 20 people were trained there), Smolensk and the Zhirovitsky monastery. On April 15, 1943 the second theological-pastoral and psalmist-singer courses began their work in Minsk. The courses worked for six months. In April 1944 22 candidates for the priesthood were prepared, four of them received priest certificates [19]. In addition, the Grodno diocesan administration issued a circular, according to which all those who wished could go with missionary activity to the eastern regions to fight against the godlessness that prevailed there under the Soviet regime. Volunteers were sent to the city of Minsk at the disposal of Metropolitan Panteleimon [4].

In total, from 1941 to 1945, 213 people were ordained a priest in Belorussia. But there were also so-called self-svyatis - "priests" who ordained themselves [70, 1. 51, 52].

With the consent and permission of the Belarusian Central Rada[1] in 1944 it was planned to open theological seminaries with a six-year course of study. In the first place - "to open half and sixth grades".

The resumption of church services in the occupied territory of Belarus happened relatively quickly. For example, the first service in Minsk after the beginning of the war was held in the Transfiguration Church of the Spaso-Preobrazhenskaya Church of the nunnery of the same name in July 1941 [16].

It was necessary to have permission from the occupation authorities to build or rebuild a church. As a rule, parishioners appealed to Archbishop Philotheus, and he - to the General Commissariat of Belarus, where this issue was finally solved.

In January 1942, by order of the clergy, Archimandrite Seraphim (Shakhmut) and priest Grigory Kudarenko were sent to Eastern Belorussia to organize church life. (More about the fate of this missionary can be read: Krivonos F. Zhitie priest-martyrs of Minsk diocese (1st half of XX century). - Minsk, 2002. - C. 115 - 165.)) We will only point out here that already in our days Fr. Seraphim was numbered among the saints as a new martyr.

[1] **BCR** (Belarusian Central Rada) - an auxiliary advisory body that operated in the occupied territory of Belarus. It was established in December 1943 by the Rada under the General Commissariat of Belarus. The BCR consisted of 14 persons, Radoslaw Ostrowski - the president. Formally Hitlerites gave the BTR the management of school affairs, culture, social care and the Belarusian Regional Defense. In reality, the Germans held the power.

Photo. The building of the cathedral in Polotsk destroyed during the Nazi occupation. Photo from the BGAKFFD funds.

Photo. Ruins of the temple in Zhlobin.
Photo from the GAKFFD funds.

During their stay in Vitebsk, Mogilev, G omel, and Minsk regions, Archimandrite Seraphim (Shakhmutya) and priest Grigory Kudarenko conducted more than ninety different services [3]. Having returned to Minsk, Archimandrite Seraphim and Fr. Gregory served in the church in honor of the Holy Spirit (now the Holy Spirit Cathedral), which they had opened. A monastery was rebuilt at the church. In June 1944, Archimandrite Seraphim and Fr. Gregory came to Grodno, where they spent much time in hospitals, giving communion to the wounded.

11

In Grodno they were arrested in September 1944.

In total, about 120 parishes were opened in the Minsk diocese in 1941, which was 30% of their pre-revolutionary number.

By 1943 there were 20 Orthodox churches in Bobruisk district, which had priests and held services [13].

In Vitebsk by June 1941 there was not a single functioning church. All churches in Vitebsk and in 11 counties had been closed before 1930. Many closed churches were turned into warehouses. An anti-religious museum was set up in one of the churches, where the relics of St. Euphrosyne of Polotsk were kept.

Photo. General view of the church destroyed by Nazi invaders in the town of Ushachi, Vitebsk region.

Photo from the funds of the BGAKFFD.

In August-September 1941 the Holy Protection Church was put in order. The first service was held on October 14, 1941. The Vitebsk Cathedral was to be repaired from the fall of 1943, but it was prevented by the war. In total, during the German occupation in all counties of the former Vitebsk province, in the cities of Nevel (now Pskov region), Velizh (now Smolensk region) Orthodox churches began to operate [1, p. 91].

There were three congregations in Mogilev. Church districts were created in the cities. There were ten congregations in Orsha, seven in Shklov, and twenty-one in Borisov [23, pp. 203-204].

In 1943 over 78 parishes were opened throughout Belarus. And for the first months of 1944 only in Minsk diocese 5 parishes were opened [19]. On February 13, 1944 a newly built church in the Minsk suburb of Kozyrevo was solemnly consecrated in the name of St. Nicholas.

Photo. St. Nicholas Church in Kozyrevo in 1944.
Photo from the author's personal archive.

A huge number of baptisms and weddings took place in the newly opened churches. In the first three or four months of the occupation of the city.

About 22,000 children were baptized in Minsk. Priests married 20-30 couples at a time [1, p. 87]. Unfortunately, the photos of 1941-1944 have not survived, but later photos allow us to imagine how it was.

Photo. During the sacrament of marriage in the cathedral in Grodno,
Photo 1946 from the author's personal archive.

Most of the parishioners went to confession. During archdiocesan services, Minsk churches were so crowded that it was impossible to raise one's hand to cross oneself.

Almost every newly opened church created voluntary committees to help the poor and war victims. In Minsk every church transferred 10% of its income to help the poor [18]. And in the Bobruisk district, 2% of the total profits of all churches and voluntary donations from believers were transferred monthly to the "Widows and Orphans Fund", which helped widows and orphans and families of priests exiled by the Soviet authorities [13]. In Minsk Archimandrite Seraphim (Shakhmut) headed a missionary committee, which spiritually cared for refugees and the sick. Two priests of this center worked in orphanages and hospitals. Divine services were also held in prisoner-of-war camps. Sometimes these services resulted in the tonsure of prisoners of war as monks.

A workshop for the beautification of churches appeared in Minsk. And in November 1943 the Minsk Historical Museum transferred through the priest Nikolai Lapitsky to the Belarusian Orthodox Metropolis in Minsk a church collection of thirty-three items [83, l. 15, 17].

Church life was especially revitalized before the feasts. Women and church choirs were involved in the preparatory work. Already in November 1941 the choirmaster of the Belarusian Theater M.I. Nikolaevich organized the Metropolitan choir, which included the best singers of the choir of the opera group of the Minsk Belarusian Theater [88, l. 22]. In the

Peter and Paul Cathedral in Minsk there was a children's choir, in which about thirty children sang. In 1944 Epiphany was widely celebrated. Unfortunately, the author does not have photos of 1944, but later photos allow us to imagine the number of participants of the Way of the Cross.

Photo. The procession to the Neman River in Grodno on Epiphany in 1946.
Photo from the author's personal archive.

During the period of occupation there was a revival of monastic life. The central place in the church activity of military Belarus was occupied by the Zhirovitsky Holy Dormition Monastery. In May 1945 there were 25 monks living in the monastery [93, 1. 7].

Photo. View of the Zhirovitsky Monastery of the Assumption of the Blessed Virgin Mary.
Photo of 1946. From the funds of the BGAKFFD.

During the German occupation resumed its work Spaso-Preobrazhensky female monastery (August 17, 1941) and Holy Spirit male monastery (May 15, 1942) in Minsk, Lyadansky male monastery (1942) [110], Spaso-Eufrosinievsky female monastery (1942) in the city of Polotsk. With the permission of the German authorities, on October 23, 1943 from Vitebsk in the Spasskaya church of this ancient Polotsk monastery were returned relics of the Monk Euphrosyne [111, p.75]. Abbess Eleutheria (Novikova) was the abbess of the monastery [96, l. 278].

Photo. Spaso-Preobrazhenskaya church of the Spaso-Euphrosynievsky nunnery in Polotsk in 1944.

Photo from the funds of the BGAKFFD.

The nunnery of the Nativity of the Blessed Virgin Mary, located in Hrodna, was also functioning. [39, л. 5]. For a very short time resumed its activity Chenkovsky monastery in the Gomel region. It was opened by Archimandrite Seraphim (Shakhmut) and Father Gregory Kudarenko. They gathered 30 sisters who elected Nun Polixenia as abbess. Archimandrite Seraphim tonsured Manefa (Skopicheva) [117, p. 157]. Unfortunately, there is no data about the number of nuns, nor about the economic activity of the monastery. It is known only that as a result of punitive expeditions of the occupiers in September 1943 in the Cenkovo monastery burned two churches and residential buildings, the nuns were dispersed, the property was looted. The candle factory at the monastery was also burned [90, l. 21].

At the end of May 1944, in view of the approaching Soviet Army, all Belarusian Orthodox hierarchs gathered in Hrodna. At the same time they transferred the relics of the holy infant martyr Gabriel of Bialystok from the Spaso-Preobrazhensky Nunnery in Minsk. In July 1944, by order of the occupation authorities, the entire Belarusian episcopate left the borders of their homeland and found themselves in a foreign land, initially in Germany, and then, the surviving Belarusian bishops dispersed throughout the world, staying in the bosom of the Russian Orthodox Church Abroad.

With the restoration of Soviet power in the BSSR, the arrests of those clergymen who were found to have connections with the occupation authorities began.

In September 1944, in accordance with the Decree of Patriarch Alexy (Simansky) of Moscow and All Russia, Archbishop Vasily (Ratmirov) took over the administration of the Belarusian dioceses.

Photo: Archbishop of Minsk and Belorussia Vasily (Ratmirov).
Photo from the author's personal archive.

By June 1945 there were three monasteries in Belarus: in Grodno - women's monastery of the Nativity of the Blessed Virgin Mary; in Zhirovitsy - men's Holy Assumption; in Polotsk - women's monastery of the Savior Euphrosynievsky [91, l. 75].

After the liberation of Belarus from the occupants, the specially created state Commission of the BSSR to assess the damage caused by the German fascist regime received 62 acts, where it was certified about the damage to the Orthodox churches in the amount of 86 091 230 rubles [89, l. 6].

Photo. Panorama of the town of Shklov, Mogilev Region, on the day of liberation on June 28, 1944. Photo from the BGAKFFD funds.

In the words of Archbishop Athanasius (Martos): "The Church consists not only of the clergy. By the Church must be understood the union of all people, both spiritual and secular, united by a living faith in Christ God, holy sacraments, church hierarchy and mutual love in Jesus Christ" [63, p. 126]. Many years of struggle of the Bolsheviks with the Church could not destroy people's desire for faith. Orthodoxy for many centuries has been the spiritual support of society, many times helped to survive the hardships. The Great Patriotic War was no exception. The fact that the faith is alive, showed the mass opening of churches. The Church, in spite of everything, survived, it was shown by the fairly rapid restoration of parish life in occupied Belarus. Archbishop Athanasius (Martos) gave a special role in the church revival to Belarusian mothers, who have always been bearers of Christian customs and traditions.

The Soviet authorities did not at all seek to create favorable conditions for the activities of the Orthodox Church. In early October 1944, a republican meeting on agitation and propaganda was held in Minsk. Speaking before the party activists, P.K. Ponomarenko said: "Churchmen expanded their activities in the liberated territories. Priests are trying to restore religious signs in the people. There are attempts to expand their influence. Comrades, the practice of all kinds of cults and our religious tolerance cannot be mixed. Let them exist, the popes, but we must take care that the popes do not become a figure on whom the supplies or spring sowing will depend" [71, 1. 239-240]. And the whole policy of the Soviet authorities in the liberated territories was aimed at reducing the influence of Orthodoxy on the population.

Photo. Bishop of Grodno Varsonofii (Grinevich). Photo of 1946 from the author's personal archive.

The period of the Great Patriotic War was a hard test for the Belarusian people. During the Nazi occupation there was a revival, and in Eastern Belorussia - restoration of church life, it was a period of opening and repairing churches, resumption of church services and revival of monasteries. It was a difficult time when every shepherd had to strengthen the spirit of his parishioners to the best of his ability, convincing them of the imminent liberation of the country.

Chapter 2

Patriotic activity of the Orthodox clergy during the Great Patriotic War

Each of us has a place on Earth that we call our homeland. For some of us it is the whole country, for others it is a small town, a village, a place. But for everyone the notion of Motherland, Fatherland is sacred. And the desire to protect or liberate our homeland from the enemy is genetically inherent in each of us. The twentieth century brought mankind two world wars that changed the course of history. The Orthodox Church in all centuries blessed the defense of the Fatherland. Back in 1813, St. Philaret of Moscow told his flock: "Avoiding death for the honor of faith and freedom of the Fatherland, you will die a criminal or a slave; die for faith and the Fatherland - you will take life and crown on yourself" [120, p. 73] [120, c. 73].

St. Righteous John of Kronstadt wrote about love for the earthly fatherland: "Love the earthly fatherland.... But especially love the heavenly fatherland. That fatherland is incomparably more precious than this one, because it is holy and righteous, incorruptible. This fatherland is earned for you by the priceless blood of the Son of God. But to be members of that fatherland, respect and love (its) laws, as you are obliged to respect and honor the laws of the earthly fatherland" [120, c. 73].

With the beginning of the occupation of the territory of Belarus, the partisan and underground movement emerged. The people of our country rose up to fight the Nazis and their servants. The first partisan detachments were formed in the summer of 1941, and 1943 went down in history as a turning point in the course of the Great Patriotic War and the Second World War as a whole. It was the second stage of mass deployment of partisan and underground struggle and anti-fascist movement on the territory of Belarus. It was reflected in the creation, development and merging of partisan zones and edges. By the end of 1943 partisans controlled about 60% of the occupied territory of Belarus [105, p. 371]. By the end of the same year the power of the occupiers, according to military historians, mainly held only in cities and along railroad lines. In Vitebsk region one of the large partisan zones was Ushachsko-Lepelskaya. It occupied 3,245 square kilometers with a population of 73 thousand people. And Borisov-Begoml partisan zone in Minsk region occupied an area of about 6 thousand square kilometers with 1 088 settlements. About 14 thousand partisans operated on this territory [105, p. 374].

The beginning of the partisan movement in Belarus posed a difficult problem for Orthodox clergymen: whether or not to support the partisan and underground movement, and how to carry out their pastoral activities in the conditions of war, occupation and confrontation between the sides.

The Nazis allowed the existence and activities of Orthodox parishes only within the framework of strict control. And in no way was the patriotic position of the Church to be manifested. Undoubtedly, during the occupation there were examples of cooperation of individual clergy with the Germans, but not these examples characterize the general attitude of the clergy and churchmen to the aggressors - occupiers. And now it is obviously time to restore justice. We can already speak and write in full voice about the cooperation of the Belarusian Orthodox clergy with the partisans and underground fighters, about their contribution to the common Great Victory, which was not widely known before. The people did not accept the "new order" and rose up to fight. Many representatives of the Orthodox clergy not only supported the partisans and underground fighters with prayers, but also provided effective assistance. The clergy mostly shared the fate of their parishioners, fulfilled their pastoral duty in a difficult hour and thought not about themselves but about others, thought not about the present but about the future, became true patriots of Belarus. The sorrow for the repressions suffered by the Soviet authorities towards the clergy did not overshadow the awareness of the general misfortune that came to the Belarusian land with the beginning of the Nazi occupation.

Undeniable, in our opinion, is the fact that a significant part of the Orthodox clergy did not accept the occupation power and were loyal to the partisan and underground movement, following the guidelines of the Moscow Patriarchate.

"Let your local partisans be for you *(believing people - S.S.)* not only an example and approval, but also an object of constant care. Remember that every favor rendered to a partisan is a merit to the Motherland and an extra step towards your own liberation from fascist captivity," wrote the future Patriarch, Metropolitan Sergius (Stragorodsky) in January 1942, "Remember that the Motherland does not forget you. So, dare, stand courageously and steadfastly, containing faith and fidelity, and see salvation from the Lord! The Lord will fight and will fight for us" [102, c. 12].

In his Christmas message of December 13, 1942, Patriarch Sergius pointed out, addressing archpastors and the population of the occupied territories: "A participant in guerrilla warfare is not only one who attacks enemy units with a weapon in his hands. A participant is also one who supplies the partisans with bread and everything they need in their life full of danger; who hides the partisans from traitors and German spies; who goes after the wounded and so on. Do not let the enemy feel himself master of your area, live in it nourished and safe. Let the rear for him be no better than the front, where our Red Army crushes him" [102, p. 39-40].

Vera Petrovna Makhnach, now a resident of Minsk, graduated from a special school in 1942 and as part of a sabotage group was thrown into the Zhlobin district of the Gomel region. Among a large number of printed publications that the group took with them were the messages of Metropolitan Sergius. They were handwritten and distributed throughout the villages. These small sheets were for many inhabitants of occupied Belarus a great moral support, an indicator that they were remembered and prayed for their liberation. The underground woman remembers that the priest of the village of Perevichi collected food for the orphanage. Maybe the old residents of this village will help to remember and return one more name of the priest-patriot.

Given the changes in the policy of the Soviet state towards the Orthodox Church, some commanders of partisan units in partisan zones encouraged the opening of churches, invited priests, and allowed the erection of roadside crosses. They did this, in most cases, for propaganda purposes, to show loyalty to the Church on the part of the Soviet authorities and thus also to make the local population understand that joining the partisan units would not lead to their excommunication from the Church. But there are also facts of quite conscious conversion to God and open recognition of His Holy Church. Thus, according to a German police report, in one of the newly opened churches in the partisan zone arrived partisan detachment, and its commander addressed the congregation gathered in the church with the following words: "In the name of the Father, and of the Son, and of the Holy Spirit! Brothers and sisters! God is and will be! We have been temporarily stupefied because we neglected God. God needs to be prayed to. Pray for us and for all the fighters and partisans. Amen!" [108, c. 96].

The ordinary clergy did not openly oppose the partisan and underground movement in Belarus. Some clergymen knew about the existence of partisan units, but did not give out their location or the names of persons connected with the partisans, although they did not always help them. Parish priests were very closely connected with their parishioners through the Sacrament of Confession. While in the cities the clergy, even in the case of sincere desire, could not actively help the partisans, in rural parishes, especially remote ones, assistance to the partisan units by priests was a widespread phenomenon.

Parish priests were often visited by partisans and police. The slightest mistake in a priest's behavior could lead to his death, both at the hands of the punishers and the partisans. Priests who helped partisans and underground fighters, well understood that they were jeopardizing not only their lives, but also the lives of their loved ones. In their pastoral ministry, the priests were guided by the words of Holy Scripture: "Whoever goes to war against us on the Sabbath day, let us fight against him, lest we all die as our brothers died in secret refuges" (1 Macc **2** 41). "For it is better for us to die in battle than to see the calamities of our people and sanctuary" (1 Macc **3** 59) - these words became for many pastors who remained in the occupied territory of Belarus a kind of motto in their ministry.

The forms of assistance varied widely: priests supplied the partisans with food, medicines, provided shelter for rest, treated the wounded, obtained documents, wrote fictitious certificates, sheltered young people, participated in reconnaissance operations, and even fought with weapons in their hands. Orthodox priests did not join partisan units en masse, but there were isolated cases.

Priest Anatol Gandarovich from the village of Rabun, Vileisky district, Minsk region, hosted partisans more than once; he received no assignments from them, but gave them food and a place to rest. The partisans kept tol, capsules and bikford cords in the priest's house. The priest also helped with medicines [3]. Anatoly Anatolievich Gandarovich was born in 1910 in the place Ilya of Vileysk district of Minsk region in the family of a clerk. When the occupation began, he was offered to work in the district administration as a bookkeeper. But the young man learned that Bishop Philotheus (Narko) had come to Minsk. Anatoly went to him in February 1942 to ask permission to pass the examinations for a priest and to be ordained. The parents of the future Archbishop Philotheos lived in the village of Ilya, his father Evdokim was a psalmist and then a deacon of the Ilya church. Before Vladimir (in monasticism named Philotheus) left his parents' home to study at the theological seminary, Anatoly knew him well. At an audience in Minsk, the request was granted. After the ordination, Anatoly was sent to the place Kraysk, Logoisk district, Minsk region. On the second day after his arrival the priest was ordered to report to the chief of the gendarmerie, who obliged Father Anatoly to report daily for a month, and then twice a month. The priest was hiding Piotr Pavlovich Maltsev, who had escaped from the Molodechno prisoner-of-war camp and lived in his house from October 1942 to August 1943, and then went to the partisan detachment "Boets" of the Frunze Brigade. Father Anatoly knew all the partisans from his village, in which house they stayed, but did not denounce them. He was arrested in February 1946 in the town of Vileika, and in October of the same year the Tribunal of the Interior Ministry sentenced the priest under Article 63-1 of the Criminal Code of the BSSR to 10 years of correctional labor camps with the loss of rights for 5 years. He was rehabilitated in June 1964.

The priest of the village of Massoliany, Berestovitsky district, Grodno region, Anatoly Miseyuk repeatedly transferred food for the partisan detachment "Zvezda", first through the liaison officer of the detachment Ivan Kolosnikov, and then, after his arrest, through the company commander of the same partisan detachment Nikolai Shishkin transferred eggs, lard, bread, moonshine to the partisans [4]. Father Anatoly was born in 1917 in the village of Staraya Rudnya, Gorodnyansky district, Chernigov province. His father Ivan Stefanovich was first a psalmist, then was ordained and served in the Starorudnyanskaya church. Besides Anatoly, there were three other sons in the family - Evgeny, the eldest, Ivan and the youngest Vitaly. In 1923 the family left for their homeland in the village of Mezhevichi (then the territory of Poland). In 1925, the father became a priest in the village of Derechin. In 1929, young Anatoly entered the gymnasium in the town of Bielsk, and four years later transferred to the gymnasium in the town of Drohiczyn nad Bug. In 1939 he received his matriculation certificate. After graduating from the gymnasium he taught the Law of God in schools. In May 1939 he married Savich Zinaida Viktorovna. In 1940 they had a son Avenir, and in 1944 - Svyatoslav. In September 1939 Anatoly decided to go to Vilna to enter the medical faculty of Vilna University, but he studied only one month. After the September events of 1939 Vilna region together with Vilna passed to Lithuania, and Anatoly returned to his family who lived in Western Belorussia. Upon his return, he was appointed by the Sokolkovo District Education Department as an elementary school teacher in the village of Yurovlyany and was immediately sent to a one-month course, upon completion of which he was appointed principal of the elementary school in the village of Garkavichi, Sokolkovo District, where he worked until the beginning of the Great Patriotic War. In the summer of 1941, Anatoly moved with his wife and one-year-old son to his father in the village of Derechinok, where his father had a parish. Anatoly began to help his father in the church, and in January 1942 he received the rank of deacon. In July-September 1942 Deacon Anatoly passed the examinations for the rank of priest at the Bialystok-Grodna Consistory in Grodno and on September 21 of the same year was ordained a priest by Archbishop Venedikt (Bobkovsky). Fr. Anatoly continued to work as a psalmist under his father until January 1943. It was then that he received an assignment to the Massolian church. To Father Anatoly the partisans came on the recommendation of the local people, who were confident in their pastor. The priest never refused the people's avengers. Partisans of the detachment together with Nikolai Shishkin came to the priest before and after the mission to rest. In the house of the priest they were fed [4]. The leadership of the partisan detachment "Zvezda" priest Anatoly Miseyuk was issued a certificate that he helped the partisans of the detachment with food, and that on his part "treacherous deeds and cooperation with the occupants" was not noticed [4]. It should be noted that the partisan command was extremely reluctant to issue such certificates. This was due, in the author's opinion, to the practical implementation of the policy of militant atheism.

The period of occupation was a very difficult and contradictory time. Every day anyone in enemy territory risked his or her life. The occupation authorities obliged all clergy, Catholic and Orthodox, to read the orders of the military and civilian occupation authorities in the churches. Father Anatoly was forced to do so as well. But despite the fact that he read out in the church in April 1943 the order to mobilize young people to work in Germany, the priest hid young parishioners, risking not only his life, but also the lives of his family. The Great Patriotic War ended, but Father Anatoly's trials were not over. He was arrested by the NKVD on November 30, 1945 and imprisoned in Grodno Prison No. 1. The priest was accused of links with the German authorities and punishers, anti-Soviet complicity and uttering "sermons of anti-Soviet character" [4]. He was tried by a military tribunal. Neither the testimony of partisans and certificates of partisan command, nor the testimony of parishioners, those whom the priest had saved the life, alleviated the fate of the priest. Father Anatoly, despite lengthy interrogations, which lasted from ten in the morning to one o'clock in the morning, did not plead guilty. The case was sent for further investigation several times. On December 4, 1946, the Judicial Board of Criminal Cases of the Grodno region sentenced him under Article 72b of the Criminal Code of the BSSR and Article 64 of the Criminal Code of the BSSR to seven years of corrective labor work with a three-year loss of rights. On the same day Father Anatoly wrote a complaint to the Supreme Court of the BSSR, but on January 3, 1947, the Judicial Board of Criminal Cases of the Supreme Court of the BSSR left the sentence unchanged.

Father Anatoly did not return to his homeland after his stay in the camps. The last place of his residence known to the author is the city of Riga. Father Anatoly was rehabilitated on July 31, 1992. Did the young man, the young pastor, who was 25 years old at the time of his ordination, know what awaited him? Of course not.

But undoubtedly he realized that he could not stay away from the events that were happening around him. And the fact that it was the parishioners who recommended to the partisans that they should not be afraid to visit the priest shows that they trusted him.

The Yassievich brothers Afanasy, a psalmist, and Georgy, a priest of the village of Sidelniki, Svisloch district, Grodno region, also hosted partisans. Beginning in 1942, partisans who called themselves "Muscovites" came to them systematically at intervals of a week or two. In 1943, on Easter Eve, about ten partisans visited the Yassievichs' house. After having dinner, one of them handed the priest a typewritten proclamation by Archbishop Nicholas (Yarushevich). "The enemy is subjecting our shrines, the temples of God, to desecration. In many towns and villages they have been turned by the fascists: into stables, into latrines, into kitchens, into torture chambers where they torture the arrested.... The Holy Church rejoices that people's Heroes - the Glorious Partisans - are rising up for a holy cause. Dear brothers and sisters! You all the holy Church fervently calls: help, what you can to these heroes to fulfill their holy act", - read the priest [42]. At the same time Athanasius gave the partisans 100 German marks and a pair of underwear [4]. The fate of this man is dramatic. He was born in Volyn in 1890 in the family of a psalmist. From 1908 to 1912 he studied in Zhitomir seminary, after which he worked as a public teacher in the town of Mtsensk for one year. His brother Georgy served in Mtsensk as a priest. Until 1922 Athanasius lived with his brother and was a psalmist in the church. In 1934 his brother was transferred as a priest to the church in the village of Sidelniki, Svisloch district, and Afanasy followed him. During the whole occupation the brothers lived together in the village of Sidelniki: George was a priest, and Afanasy was a psalmist. In 1945 Afanasy was ordained and sent as a priest to the village of Novy Dvor, Porozovsky district, Grodno region, and in 1946 he returned to Porozovo. During the occupation the brothers tried to save their parishioners by any means. In their house found shelter Popova Ekaterina Alekseevna, the wife of a Soviet officer, who did not have time to leave for the rear. In June 1942 Afanasy invited her to live in his house. There she stayed the whole occupation, in 1944 in the city of Ufa Ekaterina Alekseevna found her husband in the hospital - Suzdaltsev Fedor Vasilievich - and in January 1945 she left with him to the city of

Chkalov. Living in the house of the priest, Popova was a witness to everything that was happening. Not only partisans, but also punishers and police officers came to the house. This was the specificity of the occupation period. Nevertheless, Afanasy Yassievich was arrested in 1951, accused of close ties with the gendarmerie and anti-Soviet propaganda. Like many clergymen arrested after the war, he was not helped by the testimony of Popova, who denied the facts of his anti-Soviet activities, but claimed that the priest Afanasy knew that she was the wife of a Soviet officer and that partisans often came to the house. In December 1951, Afanasy Yassievich was sentenced to 25 years imprisonment in a special camp of the Ministry of Internal Affairs and confiscation of property. He served his sentence in Angarlag, Irkutsk region. He was released in June 1956, and in September 1992 was rehabilitated for lack of corpus delicti.

Nikolai Alexandrovich Khiltov, a priest of the village of Blyachino, Kletsky district, Minsk region, constantly helped the reconnaissance group commanded by Mikhail Shershnev from the Vasily Ivanovich Chapaev Brigade, which operated in the same region.

Photo. Priest Nikolai Khiltov with his family. The 30s of the twentieth century.
Photo from the funds of the Kletsk Local Lore Museum

In the fall of 1942, after completing a mission, a subversive group of five partisans stopped at the house of Father Nikolai. And at that time the Germans came to the village. The priest had to lock the partisans in one of the rooms of the house, and in the other to receive the punishers, who, after a short stay left. The priest provided Mikhail Shershnev with "western" clothes, got him a pass and a passport, more than once saved the commander of the subversive group, passing him off as his nephew. Father Nicholas repeatedly pointed out the location of police ambushes. In November 1942, during a firefight with the punishers partisan scout Nikolai Anokhin died. His body was brought to the house of the priest, Father Nicholas performed funeral rites over him, after which the partisan was buried in the threshing floor of the priest. After a while the partisans reburied the scout in the center of the village of Blyachino [109].

January 4, 1944, Father Nicholas Khiltov wrote a letter to the commander of the partisan detachment Eremenko from the same brigade, congratulated him on Christmas and asked him to send him Misha Shershnev, who was going through the death of his commander N.A. Anokhin, in a "rest home for the physically and mentally ill. This "rest home" was created by Father Nicholas at the church house, where the partisans improved their health [42].

The memories of the priest's daughter, Nadezhda Nikolaevna Khiltova, a former math teacher at the Sadowskaya secondary school in Kletsky district, Minsk region, have been preserved. Reading them is like hearing a voice from the past:

"My father, Nikolai Alexandrovich Khiltov, and my mother, Natalia Ivanovna Khiltov, née Novitskaya, as well as my uncle Georgi and aunt Lida, née Lidia Alexandrovna Volosovich, were arrested by the Nazis in 1944 and tortured in the concentration camp "Koldychevo" for their connection with the partisans. Our house was a turnout for the partisans. It was convenient for them that my father was the priest of the Blyachinskaya church. Because of this, our family seemed to arouse less suspicion among the enemies. Still, the frequent, mostly nocturnal visits of the partisans put our family in great danger. All members of the family knew and understood all this, but nevertheless none of the relatives spoke out in favor of ending these connections. Hatred for the enemies of the Motherland was far greater than fear of them.

In 1942, I was 14 years old and my sister Kira was 11 years old. I remember that in those war days there was constant talk about the partisans in our home. They were called "Yereminians", "Parfominians", "Zhukovians", "Dunaevians", "Shestopalovians".

There were nights when as soon as the partisans left, the local police would knock on the door. One night was particularly memorable for its anxiety. At first, that is, from the evening, there were "Zhukovtsy", as soon as they left, the police came to the house, and after them came Grisha Kuznetsov (a machine gunner).

Many of the partisans needed medical help. My mother did bandages if necessary. I helped. Dad was often sick, and Mom had to learn some of the techniques of treatment. I remember an incident when we had partisans and one of them had a wounded hand. The bullet was sitting lodged in the palm of his hand. It needed not just a bandage, but an operation. Mom, inexperienced, was afraid to remove the bullet herself. So she only bandaged his hand, and the rest was done in the partisan unit.

I remember how Alyokhin, Gordievich and Tikhanovich, who had fled from Kletsk, were hiding with us. They were teachers at the secondary technical school, which was opened under the Germans in Kletsk. They escaped in a car stolen from the German fire department in Kletsk. A chase was organized after them. The car was destroyed and these people had to escape, so they hid in our house. Later they were transferred to the partisans, but I don't remember exactly which unit. As far as I know, in 1942 in the Podishche forest near the village of Hadatovichi, partisan detachment No. 101 was created under the command of Grigory Tarasovich Drozdov, who was a military man before the war. After the war I met partisans of this detachment Nikolai Ilyukhin, who lived in the village of Uzda, and Kirill Bakhrushin. In July, the partisan detachment joined the Voroshilov Brigade and participated in the Battle of Rayevsky.

A sabotage group was operating on the Pogoreretsy-Gorodea section of the railroad. Partisans and commanders of this group - G.T. Drozdov, Nikolai Alekseevich Anokhin, Mikhail Shershnev, Grigory Trus - often visited our house. During one of the operations Shershnev Mikhail was wounded by a grenade splinter thrown by a bandit Yurka (I don't remember his surname). Grisha Trus was killed. He came from Uzda or Uzden district. It seems that he was a relative or brother of the Belarusian poet Pavlyuk Trus. Nikolai Alekseevich Anokhin was also killed while performing a combat mission in the village of Narutsevichi. Later we had a correspondence with his sister and she sent me his photo.

Mikhail Shershnev remained the commander of the sabotage group until the liberation of Belarus. Then he went to the front, was severely wounded, was treated in hospital for ten months. After the war he married and raised two daughters. I don't remember how many years ago Shershnev died of a heart attack. I corresponded with his sister. He lived at the address: the city of Nalchik, Gastello Street, 17. Former partisan Semyon Mikhailovich Bestuzhev (from the Shestopalov brigade) lives in Kherson. Radchenko Ivan Ivanovich - also a former partisan, lives in Minsk, works at the civil aviation airfield.

A former partisan commissar Pavel Fomich Volozhin kept in touch with our family. In the 1960s he was the director of the state farm "Krasnaya Zvezda" in our district for several years, and then he was transferred to work in Minsk, where he held the position of deputy minister of agriculture. We still have a letter Pavel Fomich wrote to my grandmother Nadezhda Platonovna Novitskaya in 1947. He wrote to us that no matter how difficult it was, my sister and I had to study. Later, when I studied in Minsk at the university, we met him. Kira also graduated from the university. Grandmother essentially replaced our father and mother.

Dad and Uncle Georges were arrested on the night of April 6, 1944. The date is very memorable, my sister had a daughter born on that day many years later. Mom, grandmother and we - the children stayed behind, we were not arrested purely by chance. Grandpa Khiltov was not taken either (he had throat cancer and died on April 22, 1944). There were three sons in Grandpa's family. The eldest was my father - Khiltov Nikolai Alexandrovich, born in 1903, my mother Natalya Ivanovna, born in 1907. Uncle George, born in 1905, and Uncle Sima (Seraphim), born in 1906. Grandfather Khiltov lived as a widower. Grandmother died at a young age of dysentery. Grandfather Alexander lived with his middle son Georgi. George's wife, Lydia Alexandrovna (before marriage - Volosovich), was the sister of Dmitry Alexandrovich Volosovich - former headmaster of the Krasnozvezdinskaya school. Volosovich D.A. and his wife Tatyana Petrovna were partisans during the war. Aunt Lida's father, a priest of the Iodchitsa church, was shot by the Nazis.

Mom and Aunt Lida couldn't accept it after Dad and Uncle George were arrested. They kept believing in their return. Soon my mom and I went to Baranovichi to help my dad and uncle in some way. There we met Aunt Lida. Mom and Aunt Lida left me with some acquaintances, and they went to the head of the SD in Baranovichi, Ostrovsky, hoping for his help, as he had once been Dad's teacher in Vilna. But they did not return from there.

So Kira and I became orphans (I was 16 years old at the time) and started living with my grandmother Nadezhda Platonovna Novitskaya. Our grandfather Ivan Fedorovich died back in 1929. He was a priest of the Blyachinskaya church. Before him, his grandfather or great-grandfather, surnamed Voloskovich, served in the church. Under the leadership of Novitsky's grandfather, the Blyachinskaya school was built in 1901. For this construction grandfather was awarded a diploma. It is known that the church in Blyachin was built in 1626. In 1926 its 300th anniversary was celebrated. The church was built by the landowner Mogilnitsky.

I got married in 1960. My husband - Andrey Nikolayevich Lipinsky - is Kotovsky's nephew, his mother - Tatiana Andreyevna Kotovskaya. My uncle - Efim Fedorovich Karsky - is a linguist, academician..."

In 1972, M.T. Tychyna wrote an essay about his father Nikolai Khiltov "Partyzansk batsyushka" in the magazine "Lggaratura 1 mastatstva", which is based on the memories of Semyon Mihajlovich Pestunov, a former commander of intelligence of a partisan detachment from the Chapaev brigade, which operated during the war in Kopylshchyna. Partisan recalled how after a successful diversion on the railroad "our group - five people tired from the night crossing - returned to the base in the detachment, which was stationed in the tract "Polyadi" near the village of Malaya Raevka. It was dawning in the gentile fall. We were not sure that after the operation the fascists would not organize a chase. "Let's go to Blyachino, to Father Nicholas - suggested our commander Misha Shershnev. We'll discuss, have breakfast, rest, and in the evening on the road." We looked at the commander incredulously. Misha Shershnev confidently directed his horse to the threshing-floor, opened the gate and ordered to lead the horses there, and himself, ordering us to wait, went into the house. Soon he returned with an old man, who invited us into the house with an oaky tenor, remembering the name of God, the destruction of the enemy, and that the Almighty never forgets good deeds. And all this on the fly, inviting us hospitably to pass through and make ourselves at home.

As soon as we crossed the threshold and looked around, our guide called out: "Mother, receive the guests," and opened the door to a room where we saw a woman in her forties and a girl.

Having eaten a little, we looked at Father Nicholas. Without ritual clothes, in pants tucked into cowhide boots, in a kerchief belted with a cord, he reminded us of the deacon Gavrila from the movie "Bogdan Khmelnitsky".

This is how he remained in the memory of the partisans he saved. The whole life of the family, tragic and heroic at the same time, was contained in a few pages. It is only a pity that the memory of the feat of the Orthodox priest for a long time was kept only in the memory of his daughters and in the funds of the local museum. Unfortunately, there is no memorial sign in

Kletsk, in honor of a simple parish priest, Father Nicholas Khiltov, who chose his path and walked it to the end, not spared for this life. And maybe the memorial signs, which will appear with God's help in all parishes of Belarus, where there were priests - patriots, will be the little that we can do now in memory and gratitude for their feat.

Father John Kurian, who served in a parish in the Minsk region, also cooperated with the partisans. An officer of the German army, who served as a chaplain, often came to his house and warned Father John about the forthcoming punitive actions against the partisans, and the latter, in turn, passed the information to the liaison of the partisan unit Alexander Danilovich Volohonovich [31].

Viktor Bekarevich, a priest of Latygol village, was a liaison of the partisan detachment named after Grigory Kotovsky of Vileisky district of Minsk region, later joined the partisan detachment named after Mikhail Frunze, which operated in the same region.

Photo. Archpriest Victor Bekarevich. 1980s of the twentieth century.
Photo from the author's personal archive.

In February 1944, Father Viktor Bekarevich handed over 5,100 rubles to the underground Molodechno RC of the Communist Party of the BSSR and the underground RC of the Young Communist League [45]. November 24, 1944 the headquarters of the partisan movement of the BSSR issued an official certificate to Father Viktor that he was a liaison of the partisan detachment named after Grigory Kotovsky from May 1, 1944 to June 28, 1944 [45].

Archpriest Vasiliy Kopychko, the dean of the Gomel district, was a partisan of the Vyacheslav Molotov partisan brigade, which operated in the Pinsk region.

Photo. Archpriest Vasily Kopychko. 1980s of the twentieth century.
Photo from the author's personal archive.

The priest collected information about the enemy, organized among the parishioners the collection of clothes, shoes, and food for the partisans. He distributed reports from the Sovinformburo. Father Vasily not only warned the population about the forthcoming punitive action against the partisans, but also went with the people to the partisan detachment [46].

Archpriest Mikhail Skripko - rector of the Negnevichi church of the Lida district of Grodno region, was a liaison of the partisan detachment named after Vyacheslav Molotov [46].

Archpriest Alexander Romanushko, the rector of the Malo-Plotnitsa church in the Pinsk district of the Pinsk region, participated in combat operations many times. He went on reconnaissance, was in full sense a partisan batiushka. In the summer of 1943 relatives of the policeman killed by partisans were looking for a priest for the funeral of the deceased. One priest refused, and Father Alexander agreed. An armed guard was posted at the cemetery. Everyone prepared to listen to the funeral service. Turning around the eyes of those gathered, Father Alexander, addressing the mother and father of the deceased, said: "Not our prayers and "with the saints rest" with his life deserved in the tomb the one who came. He is a traitor to the Motherland and a murderer of innocent children and elders..... Instead of "Eternal Memory" let us say "Anathema". [100, c. 14]. A dead silence was established among the astonished audience. Everything said by the priest sounded very bold and could entail his death. But Father Alexander, approaching the policemen, continued: "To you, the lost, my last request: atone before God and people for your guilt and turn your weapons against those who destroy our people, who bury living people in graves, in God's temples burn alive believers and priests"[100, p. 14]. The shocked policemen did not touch the minister of the church. The words of the priest shocked the parishioners as well. They said that if even the priests took up arms, then God Himself tells them to go to the partisans. And indeed, the guerrilla group was soon enriched with new members.

Archpriest Alexander Romanushko participated in the partisan movement from the summer of 1942 to the summer of 1944. From his letter, written in the fall of 1944 to Metropolitan Alexis, it followed that the number of priests in the Polesie diocese decreased by 55% due to the execution of many of them by the fascists precisely for assisting the partisans [27, p. 43].

More than once priests had to write certificates stating that people suspected of having links with the partisans were "deeply religious and had nothing to do with the partisan movement". By issuing such certificates to members of village councils, workers of Soviet institutions, including Soviet police officers, priests Mikhail Gaponik from the village of Devyatkovtsy, Volkovysk district, Grodno region, priest of the village of Novy Dvor, Shchuchinsk district, Grodno region, Efstafiy Balabushevich, priest of the Vladimir church in Grodno, Julian Miller saved the lives not only of partisans and underground fighters, but also their relatives [4]. Priest Mikhail Haponik was punished by the German punitive authorities for fictitious certificates with a fine of 1,000 German marks [4].

It should be emphasized that writing certificates was the most common form of assistance to the population on the part of Orthodox priests. The priest of the village of Zabrezie, Volozhin district, Minsk region, Evstafiy Baslyk, found in the church archive an old church copper (for varnish) seal with an image of a church with crosses and a Slavonic inscription in a circle: "Zabrezie St. Annunciation Church". Using this seal, the priest issued certificates that "the bearer of this, a citizen of ..., living in the village of ..., which is certified". Father Eustathius then stamped and signed. The priest issued more than a dozen such certificates, including the chairman of the Zabrezsk Village Council Ivan Vasilievich Kovalevsky, activists Ivan Staselovich and Anton Bogutsky [30].

More than two dozen such certificates were issued by the priest of Gruzdowo-Khozhowo-Polochanski parish of Maladechna district of Minsk region Mikalai Gurinovich [3]. He explained his actions simply: "I was not all-powerful and omnipotent. I was only lonely, the only one in my sincere desire to help doomed people - the only one who was not afraid to raise his voice in defense of innocent people. What I thought appropriate and necessary, at the time, I did as my heart told me to do." [3]. Reading these lines, one imagines an experienced man with gray hair. But Father Nicholas in 1941 was only 33 years old. The age of Christ. Nikolai Matveyevich Gurinovich was born in the village of Ilia, Vileysk district, in the family of a paramedic. In 1918 - 1920 he studied in the Holopenskaya gymnasium of Borisov district, Minsk province, then his parents transferred him first to the Russian gymnasium of Vileika, and then in 1923 he became a seminarian of the Vilna Theological Seminary, from which he graduated in 1930. After graduating from the seminary, the young man decided to continue his education and became a student at the theological Orthodox faculty of the University of Warsaw, from which he graduated in 1934 with the title of Master of Theology. At first Father Nicholas served in the Lublin Voivodeship, and in 1934 he was transferred to the Polesie Diocese, where he served in various parishes. In May 1940, he became rector of the Gruzdowo-Khozhowo-Polochanska church. A little over a year had passed since the beginning of his ministry at the parish when the war broke out. Being a very young man, Father Nicholas strove to make life as easy as possible for his parishioners. He wrote not only certificates, but also hid refugees in his house. The priest was not afraid to complain to the head of the district police of Molodechno Leonid Kosyak about the ugly behavior of three policemen in the temple. The priest was visited quite often by partisans, and this became known to the occupation authorities. As Father Nikolai said: "...the partisans told me that since the Germans knew that we came to you, it would be better for you to report it in order to avoid severe consequences. Which I did." Not far from the village of Polochanyi there was a camp for prisoners of war. For its prisoners in 1943, Father Nicholas conducted a food collection. In the summer of 1943, five partisans came to the house of Father Nicholas, four left, and one stayed. At that time the Germans came to the village, the priest hid the partisan in the cellar until deep into the night. The priest's wife transferred medicines to the partisan detachment. The war had not yet ended when Father Nicholas was arrested. It happened on the second day of Christmas, January 8, 1945. He was charged with the standard charge of treason against the Motherland and sentenced on April 30, 1945 to 20 years of hard labor with a 5-year term of imprisonment and confiscation of property. Nine years after the announcement of the verdict, Father Nicholas wrote a petition to K. Voroshilov for a review of the case, in which he indicated in detail how he helped not only the partisans, but also his parishioners to survive the occupation. The petition went unanswered. In 1964, the priest again wrote a complaint to the Chief Military Prosecutor's Office, and on April 10, 1965, the case was dismissed for lack of corpus delicti. 20 years of imprisonment did not break the priest in his endeavor to prove his innocence. Justice prevailed, but only 20 years of life no one can return. But for these most fruitful years of life (33 - 53 years), Father Nicholas could have done a lot of useful, carrying out service at the parish. But he had to bear a completely different cross, which he, like many others, did not suspect, but which he carried with honor.

Directly interceded for those arrested on suspicion of links with the partisans, the priest of the Hanchar church of Lida district of Grodno region Nikolai Ustinovich and the priest of the village of Olekshitsy, Berestovitsy district of Grodno region Jokim Leszczynski [4]. Fyodor Vybornov, a Grodno priest Fyodor Vybornov, did not give out the partisan liaison Elena Shemelevskaya to Zabelin's detachment. Elena Shemelevskaya used Father Fyodor's apartment to meet with the second liaison [4].

Sometimes priests managed to save the population from death. For example, the rector of the church in the village of Svetilovichi, Gomel region, John Rozhanovich, having learned about the punitive action, informed the partisans in the forest about it. Punitive actions were always accompanied by great loss of life. The first to take the blow were old men, women, children, those who lived on the border of partisan zones. This was understood by the guerrilla command. To save the civilian population, it was decided to send a church delegation to the punishers with a complaint against the partisans, emphasizing their considerable strength. The delegation asked the punishers to "protect from the bandits". The head of the delegation was Father John, who managed to convince the punishers that the villagers were not involved in the partisans and retreated [100, p. 14].

On the outskirts of the village of Hanchary, Lida district, Grodno region, one day in the summer of 1942, a firefight broke out. Frightened, the villagers took refuge in the forest.

When the partisans went into the forest, the punishers began to ask the parish priest, Father Nikolai Ustinovich, about the partisans. The priest convinced that there were no partisans in the village. Then the Germans led the priest under escort through the village, warning that if there was a single shot, the priest would be killed and the village would be burned. With an ominous escort, Father Nicholas walked through the entire village. No shots were fired, the inhabitants survived [4]. Father Nicholas at that time was not even 30 years old. He was born in 1916 in the sloboda Metera, Vladimir region, in a family of Belarusians. In 1924 the family moved to Lida, the boy went to study at the Lida folk school, in 1927 Nikolai became a student of the state humanitarian gymnasium named after Karl Khatkevich, which he graduated in 1936. The following year he became a student at the theological faculty of the University of Warsaw, where he had time to study only two courses. After the events of 1939 he returned to the city of Lida, where he worked as a secretary of the Lida branch of the Labor Guard, as a school superintendent, and as director of the children's technical station. A week after the beginning of the Great Patriotic War Nikolai came to the Zhirovitsky monastery, where he was ordained a priest by Bishop Venedikt (Bobkovsky) with the blessing of Metropolitan Panteleimon (Rozhnovsky). After his ordination he was given a place in the G onchar church. Fr. Nicholas was arrested in 1943 by the guards of the Lida-Gonchary railroad crossing and taken to a prison in a German military town on the southern outskirts of Lida. After three days he was transferred to Lida City Prison, where he was held from August 18 to September 2, 1943. Fr. Nicholas was fluent in German, and interrogations were conducted without an interpreter. The priest was tried to be accused of having links with the partisans. According to the priest, he and the commander of the partisan detachment had an agreement: in order to avoid reprisals or denunciation from neighbors, Father Nicholas could report the arrival of partisans to him after they went into the forest. After three hours of interrogation, the Germans released the priest, but on his return home they arrested him again and kept him in solitary confinement for six days without interrogation. There were grounds to suspect the priest. In 1942, the Germans arrested the fathers of partisans in Gonchary - Daineko Alexander and Mityukevich Kazimir. The relatives came to Father Nikolai for help.

After his intercession the arrested were released. The priest protected the parents of the partisans and asked for them more than once. He promised Kudele Elizaveta Yulianovna that he would protect her. During 1942-1943 the partisans systematically visited the house of the priest. Matushka prepared food, knowing that the partisans needed to be fed. In 1942 Divlyuk

Stepan Ignatyevich came to Father Nikolai and asked him to help save his relative Dikevich Nikolai Ippolitovich from being shot. In secret from everyone, the priest went to a remote farm, photographed Dikevich. Some time later, Father Nicholas managed to get documents for his namesake, and the man remained alive. For connection with the partisans arrested a resident of the v. Gonchary Kumpiak Victor Petrovich. Father Nicholas taught him how to answer questions, advised him not to confess anything. The priest went with Victor to the interrogation and waited for him in the corridor. Such attention and intercession on the part of the priest saved Victor Petrovich both from being shot and from being deported to Germany. In 1942 - 1943, on the initiative of the priest, five crosses were placed near the neighboring villages to the village of Gonchary in order to show that the local residents were Orthodox Christians. Since the fall of 1943 in the v. Gonchary was a German stronghold, and the priest maintained relations with Commandant Weitgertner. It was through him that Father Nicholas, if possible, returned passports, which were taken away by the Germans during raids. On Victory Day over Hitler's Germany, a service was held in the Gonchar church. Father Nikolai was arrested in 1950, accused of anti-Soviet activity and collaboration with the Germans. Vasiliev Nikolai Alexandrovich, during the war years he was chief of staff of the partisan detachment "Iskra" of the Kirov Brigade, at the investigation said that Father Nicholas helped the partisans, but he was not a liaison. August 14, 1950 Father Nicholas Ustinovich was sentenced to 25 years in labor camps and sent to Vorkuta. Then the term was reduced to 15, then - to 10, and then - to 7 years. At the time the sentence was announced, the priest was 34 years old.

The priest of the village of Milevichi, Zhitkovichi district, G omel region, Evgeny Krokas, actively cooperated with the Klim Voroshilov partisan detachment during the occupation and pointed out the direction of the German troops' movement. In 1943, Father Eugene read to his parishioners the appeal of the Supreme Soviet of the BSSR "To the Belarusian people".

Photo. Priest Eugene Krokas with his parishioners in 1943.

Photo from the funds of the State Museum of the History of the Great Patriotic War in Minsk.

Photo. Priest Eugene Krokas shows partisans advancing punishers,

Photo from the funds of the State Museum of the History of the Great Patriotic War in Minsk.

Many partisans needed medical assistance. Priest Boris Kirik, who served in the village of Yatra, Korelichi district, Grodno region, along with his spiritual education, also had a medical education - he was a paramedic. Father Boris dug a cellar under the floor of his church house, in which he arranged a hospital for partisans for ten beds [25]. Boris Kirik's own brother Pavel Kirik was the secretary of Bishop Athanasius (Martos) in Novogrudok. Father Boris wrote prescriptions, and Pavel Kirik received medicines according to them in the Novogrudok city pharmacy from an acquaintance of the pharmacist, the daughter of the priest Sosinovskaya. Weekly, Father Boris came to his brother for medicines [25]. To maintain the underground hospital required not only medicines, but also voluntary helpers, who were recruited from parishioners. This required from the inhabitants of the village of Yatry compliance with the rules of conspiracy, and from the priest - the talent of an organizer and great trust in the parishioners. One denunciation would have been enough to kill the entire village. These facts show that the clergymen who helped the antifascist movement had their own agent network, which is practically unknown to Belarusian researchers.

The war very sharply divided people on both sides of the barricades. On each side there were willing or unwilling participants in the war. And while clergymen who helped the partisan and underground movement were subjected to repression by the occupation authorities, priests who collaborated with the Nazis feared reprisals from the anti-fascist forces.

The partisans passed death sentences on clergymen who collaborated with the occupation regime. On February 7, 1943 priest Boris Matskevich (Rechitsa, Gomel region) and on February 21, 1943 priest Daniel Kuntsevich (parish unknown) were executed by partisan courts. Some clergymen, fearing revenge from partisans, moved to other parishes. Thus, in 1943, after the partisans killed the commandant of the German gendarmerie Naigard in the village of Novy Dvor, Radunsky district, Grodno region, priest Eustafiy Balabushevich, fearing the anger of the partisans, moved to the village of Porozovo, Svisloch district, the same region [4].

According to the information we have, 42 Orthodox priests were killed by partisans during the years of occupation. Among them: Father Anatoly Serpov, killed in 1942 (Postavy district of Vitebsk region, parish unknown), priest Vyacheslav Malashko, burned alive near the urban settlement of Begoml, Dokshitsky district of Vitebsk region in the same year. Priest Oladko was killed in Eastern Belorussia in 1942 (parish unknown), priest Anton Kalinovsky - in Valovtsy parish, Goretsky district, Mogilev region in 1943, priest Nikolai Skobei - in Polesie in 1943. In the same year the priest Nikolai Deruga was shot together with his son Veniamin [80, l. 64; 58, p. 116117]. Partisans shot Father Nikolai after he announced the decree of the German authorities about the hijacking of people to Germany. Both are buried in the village of Orlya, Shchuchinsky district, Grodno region [31].

Photo. Priest Nicholas Deruga, in 1930.

Photo from the author's personal archive.

There were cases of partisans setting fire to churches and priests' houses. For example, in the house of Father Siarhei Belaitz in the village of Yavor, Dyatlou district, Grodno region, the Germans wanted to house a police garrison. Then the partisans burned the house of the priest, and Father Sergei moved to another village, where he was repeatedly visited by the partisans. During March - April 1944 partisans burned churches in Braslavsky, Postavsky districts of Vitebsk region, in Vileysky district of Minsk region [20]. During the clearing of the territory partisans burned the church in the village of Svatki, Myadel district, Minsk region [58, p. 118].

On July 5, 1943, Father John Kushner, who had gone to meet Bishop Stephan of Smolensk to bring him to Minsk to settle church affairs, was blown up by a partisan mine. On July 8, 1943, Father John was buried in the military cemetery in Minsk. At the funeral speeches were made by Metropolitan Panteleimon, Archbishop Philotheus, Master of Theology Priest Michael Sevbo, Master of Theology Father Nikolai Lapitsky and Priest Nikifor Pysk [14].

Orthodox priests were also martyred by soldiers of the Armia Krajowa. This formation adhered to the theory of "two enemies" - Nazis and Soviet partisans. The repressions in Western Belorussia by the "Akovtsy" were mostly directed against the Orthodox population. In the parish of Tureisk, Shchuchinsky district, Grodno region, priest Ivan Alekhnovich and his mother were tortured by a Polish gang in 1942. The bandits cut off their ears, noses, gouged out their eyes, cut off the mother's breast, burned their wounds with fire and abused the victims until they died of agony. A new priest was appointed to this parish - Father Vasily,

41

who was killed on the third day after his arrival [58, p. 120].

Hieromonk Lukasz from the Zhirovitsky Monastery was assigned to a parish near the town of Novogrudok. In 1920 the Polish authorities made this parish Catholic. In 1941 it became Orthodox again. In 1942, the "Akovtsy" attacked the parish, seized Hieromonk Lukasz, buried him alive in the ground up to his neck, and on his head they built a fire [58, p. 120].

Priest Konstantin Majewski, an employee of the BNS, was killed by the bursting of a grenade thrown into his house by the "Akowskis" in 1943.

In the village of Traby, Iviebsk district, Hrodna region, bandits warned the priest Anatol Kirik that they would kill him. They motivated it by the fact that in the local Catholic parish four priests were killed in a short period of time, while the Orthodox priest was still alive. Fr. Anatoly left the parish immediately, and another priest was appointed in his place, who was familiar with the situation in Trabah, but served the parish as his priestly duty required. The shepherd was killed by the "Akovtsy" in 1943. Unfortunately, the name of this priest is not known, but we know that he was buried by Orthodox and Catholics [58, p. 120].

Archpriest Mikhail Levanchuk, rector of the parish in the village of Krevo, Smarhon district, Hrodna region, participated in the Belarusian national-educational movement during the occupation. On his initiative, a Belarusian elementary school was organized in Krevo, where the priest's daughter Larisa and a niece who came from Minsk (name unknown) worked as teachers. Father Mikhail buried all those who died at the hands of bandits according to the Orthodox rite, despite the ban. "Akovtsy" approached the house of the priest. Fr. Michael asked permission to pray before his death. The priest's daughter and niece were brought into the house, and in front of them Father Michael was shot and then the girls were also killed. The victims were buried by parishioners [58, p. 120 - 121].

Any connection with the partisans was severely punished by the occupation authorities. The Nazis not only gave permission to open churches, but also mercilessly burned them if any connection with partisans was noticed. Thus, in Drissen (now Verkhnedvinsk) district of Vitebsk region five churches were burned during punitive actions [86, 1. 22]. In October 1943 in the village of Dory, Volozhin district, Minsk region, the punishers killed 106 people, 26 of whom were driven to the church and burned alive there [26].

The inhabitants of the village of Vulka, Luninets district, Brest region, suffered the same terrible fate. All forty-seven survivors of the village, including the priest's family, were driven to the church. Shakhnovich, an eyewitness of these events, recalls that about sixty Germans broke into the church. They beat people, shot icons, then threw Molotov cocktails at the church. "Dozens of live flames rose up, high toward the cross, spoiled by smoke. A rumble went up, as if bells were ringing somewhere far away. A couple more minutes of hell in the screaming of the agonized, the fire rumbled, and golden sparks, like abundant snow, sprinkled to the floor, followed by the cauldrons. In the central dome, the flames of the central dome with their fiery scythe mowed down the gold-covered decorations and icons. They, glistening in the fire, fell down. Two carved angels placed on the ledges plunged down as if alive, with outstretched wings, breaking them as they fell. Hitting the floor, the angels shattered into pieces. Lower down, on the wall, was a large painting of the Last Judgment. With shimmering light falling on it from the brightly burning walls. The painting had been painted over a hundred years ago. The center vault above cracked, creaked and collapsed, raising a whoosh and rumble. The dome and the remains of the walls collapsed, exposing the corpses of the tortured. Having completed the "action" in this village, the punishers went on" [86, л. 72 - 74].

Photo. Priest Shasny is a witness at the trial on the case of atrocities committed by Nazi invaders. Photo from 1946. The funds of the BGAKFFD.

Priest John Loiko was the rector of the church in the name of the Intercession of the Mother of God in the village of Khorostovo, Soligorsk district, Minsk region, which was located in the partisan zone. In 1942, during the church feast after the service Fr. John blessed his sons Vladimir, George and Alexander before their departure to the partisan detachment: "My weapon against the enemies is the Holy Cross, and you be God protected and honestly serve Batkivshchina" [100, p. 7]. [100, с. 7]. In the early days of February 1943, the fascists by the forces of several field army and SS divisions, reinforced by a combined battalion of police, carried out one of the largest punitive operations to destroy partisans, and in fact the civilian population. In the Pinsk region alone, about seventy villages and fourteen Orthodox churches were burned during this operation. On February 13, the punishers completed the encirclement of the partisan zone. The partisan headquarters decided not to take the battle, but to leave the encirclement with the fewest losses. Fr. John remained with his parishioners. On February 15, the Feast of the Presentation of the Lord, the service in the church began, as usual, around six o'clock in the morning. After a while, shots were heard, and it became clear to those gathered in the church that the punishers had surrounded the village. Fr. John was told that the Nazis told everyone to go to the church to pray. Soon the church was full, but no one was allowed out of the building. Sensing the danger, the priest called everyone present to pray diligently and receive Holy Communion. While the people were singing "I Believe", the Nazis burst into the church and began to forcibly remove young women and girls from the church. Fr. John asked the officer to allow the service to end. One of the SS pushed the priest, and he fell on the royal gates. Those standing around saw nails being hammered into the doors of the church, and several sleds with straw were pulling up to the pogost. The police officers who participated in the action of destruction, testified later that from the temple already on fire was heard: "Receive the body of Christ, taste the Immortal Source" [100, p. 7]. [100, c. 7].

More than 300 charred bodies were buried in the burnt village of Khorostovo. In one of the graves burned alive priest John Lojko, peasant woman Anastasia Korzh with three small children, including one infant, Konstantin Kozlowski's family of five, 90-year-old grandfather Danilevich and many other innocent women, old people and children.

During the punitive expeditions in the Gomel region churches in the villages of Pribytki, Babichi, Larishchevo, Pokolubichi, Skitok of the Gomel district were burned [90, l. 20, 21]. During the years of occupation in the city of Gomel the Church of the Nativity of the Virgin, the newly rebuilt church of Alexander Nevsky and the cathedral with all the utensils were burned [90, l. 99].

The punishers completely destroyed churches in the villages of Zapolye, Zabolotye, Staroye Selo, Kisteni, Gadilovichi, Luchin, Tursk, Zborov of Rogachev district, and the town of Zhlobin. Many churches were desecrated before burning: floors were blown up, icons were broken [90, l. 99, 190]. In total, 21 church buildings were burned down by order of the German authorities during the years of occupation [95, l. 97].

Everything that was on the Nazi-occupied territory of Belorussia was declared the property of the Third Reich, and the Nazis made no distinction between secular and spiritual institutions. If the occupation authorities considered it necessary, churches were used as buildings for prisons and concentration camps for prisoners of war.

Photo. Former concentration camp near the walls of St. Sophia Cathedral in Polotsk, created by the Germans for residents of Polotsk and the region.

Photo of 1944. From the funds of the BGAKFFD.

Thus, in the village of Romanovichi, Gomel district, Gomel region, in the fall of 1943 in the church of St. Nicholas the Wonderworker about one hundred people were kept [95, 1. 20]. In Chechersk district of Gomel region the Germans, having looted the Spasso-Preobrazhenskaya and cemetery St. George's churches, having destroyed shrouds and about twenty icons painted by monks and painters of the Kiev-Pechersk Lavra in the eighteenth century, turned these churches into camps for prisoners of war [90, 1. 207].

At the beginning of the war, in the summer of 1941, a German military unit stopped near a church in Polesie, whose rector was Father Nicholas Mikhailovsky. The Germans wanted to camp in the church for the night, and in the altar to make a chancery with female staff. The abbot protested against such sacrilege and did not let the women into the altar. The enraged Germans attacked him, tore out his beard, mocked him, and then shot him dead. The corpse was forced to be buried at the place of execution. Only a month later the mother was able to get permission from the Germans to bury Father Nicholas in the cemetery [58, p. 122].

In the summer of 1941 there were six monks of Jewish origin in the Zhirovitsky monastery. They had taken the tonsure long ago and were universally respected. When, in June 1941, the town of Slonim and the village of Zhirovitsy were occupied by German troops, the monastery was surrounded, all the monks were ordered to line up, and monks of Jewish origin were selected from among them. Despite the requests of Metropolitan Panteleimon (Rozhnovsky), the monks were shot on the spot [58, p. 122].

Priest Ignatiy Yermolyuk was arrested by the Germans for baptizing Jews and giving them metrics, the priest was sent to a camp, from where he did not return [58, p. 122].

Priest Khodosyuk told: "In the Old Village the Germans tore up the floor, doors, windows in the church, broke the iconostasis, tore up the icons that were lying on the floor, all the utensils of the church were destroyed" [90, 1. 99] [90, л. 99].

The Nazis in the village of Teleshi, Gomel district, Gomel region, turned the church into a dumpsite, and looted the property and inventory [90, 1. 414].

If any of the priests were found to have links with the partisans, death awaited them. For example, Vladimir Nazarevsky, a priest of the Polotsk diocese, who cooperated with the partisans, was brutally tortured, and in gratitude they plowed the priest's vegetable garden at night. In the morning he was arrested. Ninety-two-year-old Father Alexander Volosovich was arrested and executed for refusing to cooperate with the occupation authorities [104].

The fates of many patriotic priests were not easy. Hieromonk Sergius from the Zhirovitsky monastery was taken to Germany to a concentration camp. His fate is unknown [63, p. 274]. The Germans took to Germany in 1943 the priest Mikhail Kashelia, the psalmist of Rakovichi church Vsevolod Ivanovich Olekhnovich [35, page 92; 36, page 29]. Known cases of relatives of clergymen were taken to Germany. In the same year 1943 the Germans sent the mother and father of the wife of the priest Nikolai Ustinovich to the camp [4].

In the fall of 1943, priest Nikolai Mikhailovsky, rector of the Holy Cross Church of the village of Rogozna, Zhabinka district, Brest region, was shot by the Germans. Against his will, a German military unit occupied the church and set up a post there. Some of the villagers were hung from the window iron bars and abused, entering the church on horses. Fr. Nicholas protested to the higher German authorities in the city of Brest. After that he was captured, the priest was forced to dig a grave in the church pogost, hung on the church fence and beaten, then almost alive knelt on the edge of the grave and shot [44].

Priest Novik with his wife and children, as well as seventy-two-year-old Archpriest Pavel Sosnovsky were shot for their connection with the partisans. After brutal torture, forty-seven-year-old priest Pavel Shcherba (parishes unknown) was also shot [58, p.122].

Fr. Kosma Raina, rector of the church in the village of Chojno, Zhabchytsky district, Pinsk region, spoke at the funeral of the executed by the Nazis inhabitants of the village of Nevel in the same district of Pinsk region: "We believe that through the prayers of the Holy Church they will receive repose with the saints, we believe that the memory of the dead will be preserved not only in our hearts, but also in the hearts of those who will be free to live on this land where their innocent blood was shed." [100].

Photo. The grave of Archpriest Kosma Raina at the Serafimovsky Cemetery in St. Petersburg.
Photo from the author's personal archive.

With the help of partisans, Father Kosma managed to join a partisan detachment and thus avoided death. Archpriest Kosma was the dean of the Pinsk western district. During the years of occupation he did not cease his divine services. As his son, Pavel Raina, recalls, in early 1942 Father Kosma was invited to his office by the district burgomaster and insistently demanded that the prayers not mention the health of the Moscow church hierarchy, and the prayer "For our country, authorities and its host let us pray to the Lord" was changed with the words: "Let us pray to God for the liberated country of Russia and the victorious German army", as it was stated in the circular of the Pinsk spiritual consistory [100]. However, the priest on Easter night of 1943 in a huge crowd of people read the address of Metropolitan Nicholas (Yarushevich) to the population of the temporarily occupied territory. In his sermon, addressing the parishioners, Father Kosma said: "...God's will is not in the decrees of the occupiers, but in the commandment of our Lord Jesus Christ to love one another and to remember always that 'there is no greater love than that love who lays down his life for his friends'." God's will is not in the orders of the fascists, but in the calls of our native Russian Orthodox Church to our believing hearts, so that in this terrible hour there would be as few hollow flowers as possible in the church field and every living heart would blossom with rays of mercy for our brothers who defend our Orthodox faith and Fatherland with arms in their hands. Brothers! Whoever you can and whenever you can, help the people's avengers in their good and great cause! And most importantly, do everything "not sighing, but always giving thanks to God, who sees all your heart and will repay you a hundredfold on your last day..." [100]. [100]. October 9, 1943 at dawn, the Nazis surrounded the village of Hoino. Fr. Kosma was in the church, he was ordered to expose himself and follow to the police station. They took away the priest's documents, saying that he would not need them anymore. Father Kosma realized that his last hour had come. Passing by the church, the priest fell to his knees and began to pray, the guards were Czechs by nationality and seeing how fervently the priest prayed, moved aside not to disturb him. As the clergyman himself recalled, he did not know how long his prayer lasted. When he rose to his feet, he saw that there was no one around. Getting up from his knees, he crossed himself and walked away in the direction of the forest. A few days before the New Year's holidays, the commander of the Kirov partisan detachment Nedelin invited the priest to take part in the New Year's rally. Here's how Father Kosma describes this event: "...In a vast clearing opposite the headquarters dugout were built by companies of partisan heroes. The chief of staff accompanying me, noticing that I was looking for someone with my eyes, understood me without words, pointed me to the scouts standing to our right, among whom I saw my sons Peter and Paul. My heart beat in indescribable joy. The New Year's rally began. And now it was my turn to say a word: "Dear brothers, we are all sons of one great Motherland, the love for which has gathered us here to celebrate the coming New Year 1944.

Not far behind us are our mothers, children and wives, who are waiting for us to protect them from the enemy, who came to take away our bread and turn all of us into slaves. But our chronicled Belarusian land has always been rich in miracle-bogatyrs.... I know that some of you have French rifles from the times of the first Patriotic War of 1812. What does that say? Our great-grandfathers also defended their home and protected it. I know that many of you have not only German automatic rifles, but also machine guns, and this shows that you are the same wonder-gods, who in the coming year, I believe, will free their native land from fascist evil. And in this great endeavor, may God help us! Happy New Year, my dears and dear ones! The last words were covered with a mighty threefold 'hurrah'." [100]. November 15, 1944, the commander of the Kirov guerrilla unit Nedelin wrote a characterization of the priest Kosma Raina, which indicated that he assisted the guerrillas operating behind enemy lines, delivered intelligence to the guerrilla units, urged the population to assist the people's avengers, showed himself as a true patriot of his homeland.

The family of the priest of the village of Lasha, Vitaly Borovsky, was shot by the Germans in the fall of 1943 for his connection with the partisans. He was betrayed by the wife of the assistant village head Maria Lyanger, who saw partisans in the priest's house. The informer did not escape retribution. The partisans shot her [4].

Priest Piotr Batsyan, who served as rector in the village of Kobylniki, Myadel district, Minsk region, was arrested by the SD for helping Jews. Fr. Peter was sixty years old. He was cruelly abused in Minsk prison: they harnessed him to a plow and plowed the prison vegetable garden, poisoned him with dogs until the priest died. In 1943 the SD shot Priest Malishevsky in the town of Slonim, Grodno region. Archpriest Pavel Sosnovsky issued certificates of trustworthiness. During the raid a man with Father Pavel's certificate was arrested, for which Archpriest Pavel was arrested by the SD and brutally tortured [58, p. 123].

Father Boris Kirik was also killed. He was betrayed by a man treated in an underground hospital, who then joined the police. Kirik died without giving up his brother and Sosinovskaya [25].

In some cases priests-patriots were honored with government awards. For services to the Motherland and for personal courage, priest (later archpriest, rector of St. Alexander Nevsky Church in the Military Cemetery in Minsk) Viktor Vasilievich Bekarevich was awarded the Order of the Great Patriotic War of the second degree [99].

For participation in the partisan movement Kuzma Petrovich Raina was awarded combat medals "For Victory over Germany" and "Partisan of the Great Patriotic War" I degree.

Father Vasily Kopychko was awarded medals "For Victory over Germany", "For Valorous Labor during the Great Patriotic War" [46]. [46].

Zashtatny Archpriest Peter Rozhanovich from the parish of the village of Rukhcha, Stalin district, Brest region, for his service during the Great Patriotic War, for the help he provided to his parishioners and local partisan units, was awarded the medal "For Valorous Labor during the Great Patriotic War" [46] [46].

Evgeny Miseyuk, a priest of the parish of the village of Omelenets, Kamenets district, Brest region (later archpriest, clachar of the St. Dukhov Cathedral in Minsk), was awarded the medal "For Valorous Labor during the Great Patriotic War" and the Order of St. Sergius of Radonezh for his patriotic work during the war years.

Photo. Priest Eugene Miseyuk. 1930s-40s of the twentieth century.
Photo from the author's personal archive.

Marshal G. K. Zhukov personally addressed to Fr. Eugene with gratitude for his service to the Motherland and in recognition of his services sent from East Prussia for the Holy Cross

Church in the village of Omelenets three church bells [43].

In 1945, Father Fyodor Slabukho, priest of the Porech church of Pukhovichi district, Minsk region, sent a letter to P.K. Ponomarenko, in which he told about his difficult financial situation. During the German occupation, Father Fyodor provided material assistance to the partisans. On the direct instruction of P.K. Ponomarenko, a food parcel was prepared for the priest, which was personally taken by Deputy Chairman of the Council of People's Commissars of the BSSR Grekova, at the same time presenting the priest with a partisan medal [95, 1. 4].

In December 1942, Metropolitan Sergius (Stragorodsky) appealed to all believers to donate funds for the tank column named after Demetrius of Don: "Let our church column bear the blessing of our Orthodox Church and its unceasing prayer for the success of Russian arms. It will give us all a consoling consciousness that we will not stand aside, that we also participate in the holy cause of the salvation of the Motherland by our strength and ability" [102, p. 42]. [102, c. 42].

Photo. Tank column named after Demetrius of Don.
Photo from the funds of the BGAKFFD.

Photo. Fighters of the tank column named after Dimitri Donskoy
Photo from the funds of the BGAKFFD.

The money for the construction of the tank column was transferred to the local branches of the State Bank to be transferred to the special fund in Moscow for the construction of the church tank column named after Demetrius Donskoy. At the same time the Moscow Patriarchate was also notified of the donations. By June 1942 more than 8 million rubles had been collected [102, p. 42]. In parallel, there were collections of warm clothes for Red Army soldiers, money for gifts to them for holidays, for the care of disabled war veterans, for the education of military children and for the restoration of areas affected by the German occupation. By the end of 1943, the total contributions of the Russian Orthodox Church to the defense fund amounted to more than 300 million rubles. Only in March 1943, the believers and laity of Belorussia, evacuated deep into Russia, and those who were in enemy-occupied territory, contributed 5,400 rubles for the construction of airplanes and armored train "Soviet Belorussia" [61, p. 169].

Belarus was quickly occupied by the enemy and could not provide monetary aid to the Red Army in full. However, during the occupation there were isolated cases of clergymen transferring money to the Red Army through partisan detachments and underground district committees of the Communist Party. Seventy-two-year-old priest Yakov Slobukho from Gressky district (now Kopyl district) of Minsk region transferred to the underground Gressky district committee of the Communist Party (b)B 200 rubles in money and 180 rubles in bonds to the country's defense fund, which was mentioned in the political report of the secretary of

52

the underground Gressky district committee of the Communist Party (b)B I. I. Puzevich to Minsk.I. Puzevich to the Minsk underground regional committee of the CP(b)B on party, mass-political work and combat activities of the underground in May 1943 [29, p.435]. And on July 28, 1943, the priest of the village of Vetly, Pinsk district, Brest region, whose name, unfortunately, is unknown, gave the commissar of the Suvorov partisan detachment Sergei Chubarev 490 rubles for the construction of a tank column [46]. The church tank column named after Demetrius of Don participated in many battles during the Great Patriotic War, gaining fame.

Active assistance to the front on the part of the Orthodox Church in Belarus began from the time of the liberation of the republic from German troops and continued until the end of the Great Patriotic War.

Already on August 24, 1944, the order of the Council of People's Commissars of the USSR allowed the State Bank to open current accounts for diocesan offices and parishes of the Moscow Patriarchate to store church funds and for donations [94, 1. 8].

Archbishop Vasily (Ratmirov), who headed the Orthodox Church in Belarus after the liberation of the republic, made many efforts to actively collect donations. While during the occupation the Orthodox clergy primarily provided prayer support to the front, from August 1944 they began to provide substantial material aid. By December 1944, the Orthodox Church in Belorussia collected 4,872,000 rubles for the defense fund of the country, families and orphans of Red Army soldiers [92, 1. 140].

On January 19, 1945 Archbishop Basil appealed to the Chairman of the Council of People's Commissars of the BSSR P.K. Ponomarenko with a request to allow the opening of a church plant. In October 1944 a factory for the production of church candles was opened at the Minsk Church Administration. Its opening pursued two goals: to satisfy the church's requests for candles and to collect funds for the country's defense fund [92, 1. 51]. But due to the fact that on the territory of Belarus there were many artisanal workshops of this profile, the sales of candles of the plant were very small. Thus, from October 1944 to January 1945 the turnover of the factory amounted to 96,000 rubles, of which 25,000 rubles were transferred to the fund to help the families of the Red Army soldiers and 15,000 - to the defense fund [92, 1. 51]. Archbishop Basil calculated that if the plant served all the churches of Belarus, the working capital would be at least 1,500,000 rubles and deductions to the defense fund would not be 40,000 rubles, but about 1,000,000 rubles [92, l. 51]. In this regard, Archbishop Basil appealed to P.K. Ponomarenko with a request to issue an order by the Council of People's Commissars of the BSSR to liquidate all illegally existing candle workshops. He argued that this would contribute to the development of the church plant, which would allocate considerable sums to the Defense Fund of the country [92, l. 52].

Archbishop Basil repeatedly addressed the faithful with messages calling for donations to be made to the country's defense fund. This had positive results. Only for the period from September 1 to December 31, 1944 the clergy of Belorussia and believers collected 2,190,473 rubles in money, food and canvas [92, l. 54]. From them in the defense fund of the country received 1 639 393 rubles and in the fund to help the families and orphans of Red Army soldiers - 551 080 rubles. In addition, Archbishop Basil personally contributed 33,000 rubles to the defense fund and 75,000 rubles to the fund for the families and orphans of Red Army soldiers. Thanks to the efforts of the Orthodox clergy, 2,300,475 rubles were collected and transferred to both funds [92, l. 54]. It was "the first modest gift, the gift of love for the Red Army, crushing now the fascist beast in its own den," - wrote Archbishop Basil P.K. Ponomarenko in March 1945 [92, l. 54]. He assured that the Orthodox Church in Belarus would continue to take "the liveliest part in providing material assistance to the Red Army in the final defeat of Nazi Germany" [95, l.98]. [95, л.98].

Material donations continued in 1945. If for five months of 1944 (from August to December 1944) in Brest region was collected for military needs 140 986 rubles and two pounds of silver coins, then in January-February 1945 the money collection for defense needs amounted to 512 627 rubles and one pound of silver coins [95, l. 98].

In the Kobrin district (archpriest F. Dmitriuk was the archpriest) 172 073 rubles were collected, in the Antopolsky district (archpriest A. Matskevich was the archpriest) - 74 760 rubles, in the Vysokovsky district (archpriest S. Dekov was the archpriest) - 59 032 rubles [95, l. 98, 118]. In addition, in significant quantities came grain, food, linen. For two months of 1945 only in the Vysokovskiy district 5 700 kilograms of grain and other products, 632 meters of cloth, 330 units of different things (mittens, socks, scarves) were handed over. In total, the clergy and believers of Brest region contributed 1,328,580 rubles and three pounds of silver to various funds in 1944-1945 [95, l. 98, 118].

The bishops of Brest region at their meeting on March 15, 1945, dedicated to the deployment of agitation and patriotic work among the faithful, decided to "tirelessly conduct patriotic work in all parishes of the diocese, maintaining the spirit of vigor among the parishioners by giving appropriate sermons from the church pulpit and private conversations, disposing parishioners to generous donations of money and in kind for the needs caused by the war, both by word and especially by personal example" [95, fol. 98]. [95, л. 98]. This attitude and position of the Orthodox clergy was observed throughout the territory of Belarus.

Abramov, a priest of the Tolochin church of the district of the same name in the Vitebsk region, did considerable work. He contributed 10,000 rubles to the Red Army fund and 12,000 rubles to help orphaned children. Slovenskaya church of the Tolochinsky district collected 8,000 rubles, Beshenkovichskaya church contributed 17,000 rubles to various funds, other churches of the Vitebsk region contributed amounts from 1,000 rubles to 5,000 rubles [95, l. 188].

From March to June 1945, the clergy and believers of Grodno region contributed to the defense fund of the country 36,484 rubles and gave in kind 282 kilograms of oats, 8 kilograms of flax. The clergy and believers of Grodno region contributed 12,958 rubles in money and 750 rubles in kind to the fund of assistance to the families of front-line soldiers and Soviet partisans [96, l. 12].

Believers of Baranovichi region (which existed until 1954) donated 65,971 rubles 45 kopecks to the defense fund, in favor of orphans and families of Red Army soldiers - 39,895 rubles, a total of 105,866 rubles 45 kopecks [95, l. 59]. The clergy also cared for the wounded, who were treated in hospitals. In early 1945, the Orthodox Church held a one-time collection of food for military hospitals and for the families of servicemen. Only in Baranavichy region 2 700 eggs, 12 kilograms of butter, 1 865 kilograms of rye, 93 meters of canvas, 2 kilograms of flax and 80 kilograms of potatoes were collected for these needs [95, l. 59].

The believers of the Pinsk region also made their contribution to the front. It existed until 1954, then it was included in the Brest region. The parishioners together with the clergy contributed 101,110 rubles to the defense fund, 51,540 rubles to the fund to help the families of the Red Army soldiers, 23,953 rubles in kind for the construction and needs of the tank column named after Dimitri Donskoy and 85,898 rubles in terms of money [95, l. 110].

The clergy also participated in the 4th State Military Loan. The priest of the church of St. George the Victorious in the town of Lida Evgeny Cheshik subscribed for three thousand rubles, urged the faithful to participate in the subscription to the loan [95, l. 4]. The priest of the village of Olekshitsy, Berestovitsy district, Grodno region, Vladimir Belyaev subscribed to 1,000 rubles and contributed this amount in cash, during the church service he congratulated the believers on the victory over Nazi Germany and urged the population to participate in the 4th State Military Loan [95, l. 4]. In total, the Orthodox clergy of Grodno region subscribed to the 4th State Military Loan and contributed 52,990 rubles to the bank [95, page 12]. The believers of the Pinsk region subscribed 12,945 rubles [95, l. 110].

If we take into account the fact that all donations were made during the difficult war days by the population that survived the occupation, then these seemingly small amounts of donations become a kind of a feat of people who put the fate of the Motherland above personal problems, realizing that in a terrible war one cannot survive alone.

The clergymen encouraged the population not only to donate by personal example. Aliaksandr Haholushka, a priest of the Rakovichi church in Shchuchyn district of Hrodna diocese, found out that the village council, where his parish was located, did not fulfill the logging plan. At the general meeting of the peasants, the priest offered his help to the village council. The priest took a saw and an axe and went to work in the forest. The news quickly spread around the parish. The population went to logging after their priest and exceeded the plan in two days [95, l. 3].

The priest of the Spasso-Preobrazhenskaya church in the village of Ostrino, Grodno region, Pyotr Golosov systematically read out the orders of Supreme Commander-in-Chief I.V. Stalin during church services and familiarized the believers with the situation at the fronts and the victories of the Red Army [95, l.3].

The hardships of the war and the period of occupation were a heavy burden on the shoulders of the population. The clergymen were not practically different in their financial situation from their parishioners. After the liberation of Belorussia and until May 1945, the Orthodox Church in Belorussia, as mentioned above, contributed about 6 million rubles and three pounds of silver to various funds [101].

In addition to monetary contributions to various funds, the Orthodox clergy subscribed to the 4th State Military Loan and contributed 65,845 rubles to the bank [101].

Understanding the difficulties faced by widows and orphans, sharing their pain, the Orthodox clergy gave them 7,857 kilograms of grain crops, 725 meters of cloth, in terms of money their help amounted to more than 85,000 rubles [101].

It can be concluded that a significant part of the Orthodox clergy actively participated in patriotic work in 1944 - 1945. Moral support was realized through their service to God and helping parishioners with prayer and consolation. The amount of material assistance to the front on the part of the Orthodox clergy of Belarus was quite significant for the wartime and undoubtedly made life easier for many people and brought the Great Victory closer.

Literature

1. Alexeev V. German policy towards the Russian Orthodox Church in the German-occupied territory of the USSR// On Themes Common and Russian. - New York, 1963. - C. 90 - 124.

2. Alekseev VA Marshal Stalin trusts the church // Agitator. - 1989. - № 10. -C. 26 - 30.

3. Archive of the State Security Committee of the Republic of Belarus.

4. Archive of the Department of the State Security Committee in Grodno region.

5. Barkan V. Will the people forgive // Sovetskaya Belorussia. - 1965. - April 7.

6. Belaruskaya gazeta. - 1942. - № 95. - 7 snizhnya.

7. Ibid. - 1942. - № 16. - March 11.

8. Ibid. - 1942. - № 39. - June 6.

9. Ibid. - 1943. - № 1. - January 7.

10.   Ibid. - 1943. - № 97. - December 18.

11.   Ibid. - 1943. -№ 15. - February 27.

12.   Ibid. - 1943. - № 23. - March 22.

13.   Ibid. - 1943. - № 47. - June 27.

14.   Ibid. - 1943. - № 52. - July 14.

15.   Ibid. - 1943. - № 56. - July 28.

16.   Ibid. - 1943. - № 97. - December 18.

17.   Ibid. - 1944. - № 7. - January 26.

18.   Ibid. - 1944. - № 15. - February 26.

19.   Ibid. - 1944. - № 23. - March 22.

20.   Ibid. - 1944. - № 24. - March 25.

21.   Ibid. - 1944. - № 25. - March 29.

22.   Belarusian Staronka. - Vshchebsk. - 1942. - № 7. - 15 traunya.

23.   Bird E. Tomas. Orthodoxy in Byelorussia: 1917 - 1980 // Zatsy. Belarus shstytut nawuy

i mastatstva. - New York, 1983. - C. 144 - 209.

24. Library of the Zhirovitsky monastery.

25. Library of the Minsk diocesan administration.

26. Volnaya pratsa (organ of Slonim RC CP(b)B). - Slonim. - 1943. - October 12.

27. Vasilieva O.Y. Russian Orthodox Church in 1927 - 1943 // Voprosy istorii. - 1994. - № 4. - C. 43.

28. All-People's Struggle in Belarus against Nazi invaders during the Great Patriotic War: In 3 vol. - Minsk, 1983-1985. - T. 1 - 3.

29. National Partisan Movement in Belarus during the Great Patriotic War (June 1941-July 1944): Documents and Materials: In 3 vol. - Minsk: Belarus, 1973. - T. 2. - C. 435.

30. Priest Evstafiy Baslyk. Notes of Priest Evstafiy. - Mn., 2005. - C. 164.

31. Memories of A.I. Kurian.

32. State Archive of Vitebsk region, f. 1431, op. 1, d. 1.

33. ibid. f. 2848, op. 1, d. 140.

34. State Archives of Grodno Region, f. 1, op. 1, d. 58.

35. ibid. 478, op. 1, d. 10.

36. ibid. 478, op. 1, d. 12.

37. ibid. 478, op. 1, d. 32.

38. ibid. 478, op. 1, d. 52.

39. ibid. 478, op. 2, d. 1.

40. Pstory of the Belarusan SSR: In 2 vol./GS.Krauchanka, N.V.Kamenskaya. - Mshsk: Academy of Sciences of the Belarusian SSR, 1958. - T. 1 - 2.

41. Pstory of the Belarusan SSR: 5 vol. - Mshsk: Navuka i tehshka, 1975. - T. 1 - 4.

42. State Museum of the History of the Great Patriotic War in Minsk, Department of Fonds, No. kp 14587, D - 82 - 62.

43. ibid., department of funds, report to Vladyka dated 17.02.48 from the parish of

Omelyanets, Brest region.

44. ibid., fonds department, message from the rector of the St. Nicholas Church in the village of Ozyaty, Archpriest John Petruchuk, May 27, 1958.

45. ibid., fonds department, f. 8915, n/a 23879-23882.

46. ibid, Dept. of Foundations, kp 35687 D-9851 Inv 35687.

47. ibid, department of foundations, kp 63215 20 - 7 - 7.

48. ibid, fonds department, n/a 71007/1 w 8, a ya 24 A-33-68.

49. ibid, Dept. of Foundations, A 33-81 w 8a, I 24.

50. ibid, Dept. of Foundations, A 33-51, ch 10 a, i 19.

51. ibid, Dept. of Foundations, A 33-72, w 8 a, i 24.

52. ibid, Dept. of Foundations, n/a 4162, 20 - 8a - 24.

53. ibid, funds department, n/a 458720 - 8a - 24.

54. Documents denounce. - Minsk: Belarus, 1964. - 270 c.

55. Dmytruk K.E. Swastika on sutans. - M: Political Literature, 1976.

56. Banner of Youth. - 1964. - July 31.

57. History of the Second World War 1939 - 1945: In 12 volumes / Edited by A.A. Grechko. - Moscow: Voenizdat of the Ministry of Defense of the USSR, 1975. - T. 1- 12.

58. Kasiak I. Z pstor'n pravoslaunai tsarkva Belaruskaga narodu. - New York: BCR, 1956. - 190 c.

59. Kanfesn in Belarus (the end of the 18th - 20th centuries) / Ed. U.1. Navshkt - Minsk: VP "Ekaperspectiva", 1998. - 340 c.

60. Korzun M.S. Russian Orthodox Church. 1917 - 1945. - Minsk: Belarus, 1987. - 111 c.

61. Kotov A. Drama of the Belarusian Church // Neman. - 1997. - № 1. - C. 155 - 174.

62. Kletsky Museum of History and Local Lore, Department of Funds.

63. Martos A. Belarus in historical and state and church life. - Buenos Aires, 1966. - C. 270 - 290; Martas A. Mataryyaly da pstoryi Pravaslaunai Belaruskai Tsarkva. - Zhyrovshchi. 2004.

64. Melnikov A. Archimandrite. Zhirovitsky monastery in the history of the Western Russian dioceses. - Odessa. 1964. - 280 c. typescript.

65. Menskaya gazeta. - 1942. - 7 snow.

66. Narysy pstoryi Belarus U 2 ch. / M.P. Kasciuk, 1.M. 1gnatsenka, U.1. Vyshynsyu 1 1nsh. - Minsk: Belarus. 1995. - Ч. 2. - 560 c.

67. National Archives of the Republic of Belarus. f. 3. op. 1. д. 1145.

68. ibid. f. 4. op. 2. д. 146.

69. ibid. f. 4. op. 29. д. 146.

70. ibid. f. 4. op. 29. д. 539.

71. ibid. f. 4. op. 47. д. 19.

72. ibid. f. 370. op. 1. д. 1.

73. ibid. f. 370. op. 1. д. 2.

74. ibid. f. 370. op. 1. д. 3.

75. ibid. f. 370. op. 1. д. 25.

76. ibid. f. 370. op. 1. д. 177.

77. ibid. f. 370. op. 1. д. 305.

78. ibid. f. 370. op. 1. д. 378.

79. ibid. f. 370. op. 1. д. 382.

80. ibid. f. 370. op. 1. д. 386.

81. ibid. f. 370. op. 1. д. 387.

82. ibid. f. 370. op. 1. д. 418.

83. ibid. f. 370. op. 1. д. 433.

84. ibid. f. 370. op. 1. д. 436.

85. ibid. f. 370. op. 2. д. 1271.

86. ibid. f. 750. op. 1. д. 239.

87. ibid. 381, op. 1, d. 2.

88. ibid. 384, op. 1, d. 177.

89. ibid. f. 861, op. 1, d. 3.

90. ibid. f. 861, op. 1, d. 6.

91. ibid. f. 951, op. 1, d. 1.

92. ibid. f. 951, op. 1, d. 2.

93. ibid. f. 951, op. 1, d. 3.

94. ibid. f. 951, op. 2, d. 1.

95. ibid. f. 951, op. 2, d. 2.

96. ibid. f. 951, op. 2, d. 3.

97. ibid. 3500, op. 2, d. 1299.

98. New Way. - Bobruisk. - 1943.

99. Poluyanov M. 60 Years of Service to the Church // Tserkvonnoe Slovo. - 1996. - № 11. - C. 1.

100. Raina P.K. We are children of one Fatherland // Slovo. - 1989. - № 11. - C. 12 - 15; Raina P. Together with miracle-godatyrs// Science and Religion. - 1995 .- № 5. - C. 7 - 8.

101. Calculations by S.V. Silova, 1999.

102. The Russian Orthodox Church and the Great Patriotic War. - Moscow Patriarchate Publishing House, 1943. - 99 c.

103. Sovetskaya Belorussia. - 1961. - April 9.

104. Ibid. - 1965. - April 7.

105. The Soviet Union during the Great Patriotic War / Edited by A.M. Samsonov. - Moscow: Nauka, 1985. - 711 c.

106. Smirnov A. Opponents of the cross of the Lord// Journal of the Moscow Patriarchate. - 1943. - № 3.

107. Statute of the Holy Pravaslaunai Belarusian Autakefalnai Tsarkva //Kasiak I. Z gyutoryp

pravaslaunai tsarkva Belaruskaia narodu. - New York: BCR, 1956. - C. 173 - 188.

108. Turonak Y. Belarus under the German occupation. - Mshsk: Belarus, 1993. - 232 c.

109. Tychyna M. Partyzansk batsyushka // Lggaratura i mastatstva. - 1972. - 14 Studzenya.

110. Churches and parishes of Minsk (history and modernity). - Minsk: Belarusian Orthodox Brotherhood of Three Vilna Martyrs, 1996. - 102 p.

111. Sheikin G. Polotsk diocese (historical and statistical review) - Minsk: Belarusian Orthodox Brotherhood of three Vilna Martyrs, 1997. - 95 c.

112. Encyclopedias of the History of Belarus in 6 vol. - Mshsk: BelEn. - T. 2. - 494 c.

113. Pospelovsky D.V. Russian Orthodox Church in the Twentieth Century. - M: Respublika, 1995. - 510 c.

114. Tsypin V. History of the Russian Church 1917-1997. - M.: Izd-wo Spasso-Preobrazhensky Vaalamsky Monastery, 1997. - T. 9, - 832 c.

115. Shkarovsky M.V. Policy of the Third Reich in relation to the Russian Orthodox Church in the light of archival materials of 1935 - 1945 years (collection of documents). - Moscow, 2003.

116. Silova S.V. Orthodox Church in Belarus during the Great Patriotic War: Study Guide. - Grodno: GrSU, 2002.

117. Krivonos F. The Lives of the Priest Martyrs of the Minsk Diocese (1st half of the 20th century). - Minsk, 2002.

118. The Third Reich and the Orthodox Church // Science and Religion. - 1995. - № 5. - C .22 - 23.

119. Resolution of the All-Russian Central Executive Committee and the RSFSR SNK of 08.04.1929 "On Religious Associations"/Investigations of the Central Executive Committee of the USSR and the All-Russian Central Executive Committee of April 26, 27, 28, 1929 - № 96, 97, 98.

120. The Russian Church at the turn of the century. Jubilee Council of Bishops of the Moscow Patriarchate. - St. Petersburg: publishing house "Tsarskoe Delo", 2001. - 319 c.

Svetlana Vladimirovna Silova. Born in Grodno, graduated from the Faculty of History of Grodno State University. In 2000 she defended her PhD thesis on "The Orthodox Church in Belarus during the Great Patriotic War", associate professor of the Department of History of Belarus at Yanka Kupala State University of Grodno. Author of the book "The Orthodox Church in Belarus during the Great Patriotic War: Study Guide."- Grodno: GrSU, 2002.

Printed by Books on Demand GmbH, Norderstedt / Germany